A Study of Performance Measurement in the Outsourcing Decision

A Study of Performance Measurement in the Outsourcing Decision

R. McIvor, P.K. Humphreys, A.P. Wall,
A. McKittrick

University of Ulster
Northern Ireland

ELSEVIER

AMSTERDAM • BOSTON • HEIDELBERG • LONDON • NEW YORK • OXFORD
PARIS • SAN DIEGO • SAN FRANCISCO • SINGAPORE • SYDNEY • TOKYO
CIMA Publishing is an imprint of Elsevier

CIMA
PUBLISHING

CIMA Publishing is an imprint of Elsevier
Linacre House, Jordan Hill, Oxford OX2 8DP, UK
30 Corporate Drive, Suite 400, Burlington, MA 01803, USA

British Library Cataloguing in Publication Data
A catalogue record for this book is available from the British Library

ISBN: 978-1-85617-680-4

For information on all CIMA publications
visit our website at www.elsevierdirect.com

Typeset by Macmillan Publishing Solutions
(www.macmillansolutions.com)

Transferred to Digital Printing 2009

Contents

Executive Summary

This book involved developing a framework, which incorporates performance measures that can be used in the outsourcing process. The outsourcing framework was applied in a UK financial services organisation over a 4 year period. The research has shown how performance measures can be established and then used to benchmark internal performance with that of service providers. In particular, application of the framework provides useful insights for organisations considering outsourcing and assists in assessing service levels throughout the contract. The research has also identified the benefits and challenges of performance management in the outsourcing process. The findings have a number of important implications for practitioners.

- Organisations must have robust performance measurement systems in place in order to effectively evaluate and manage the outsourcing process. Effective performance measurement can assist in identifying causes of poor performance prior to outsourcing. Furthermore, outsourcing processes without developing effective performance measures means an organisation will not know whether service providers are executing processes better or worse than the internal departments.

- Organisations must have a clear understanding of the relationship and inter-dependencies between business processes prior to outsourcing. Failure to understand process inter-dependencies means it will be difficult to assess the performance of individual processes independently of other processes in outsourcing arrangements.

- Although extensive process analysis is time consuming and difficult, it is a crucial element of outsourcing. Redesigning processes can enable an organisation to define clear boundaries between processes that should be internalised and those that should be outsourced. Furthermore, detailed requirements analysis can be derived from process analysis, which will facilitate the development of an effective service level agreement, which can be used to measure service provider performance.

- Linking process importance and performance capability dimensions is a central element of outsourcing. Identifying critical and non-critical processes ensures that processes that are deemed crucial to the overall performance and success of the organisation are not lost to service providers. This analysis can also serve as a valuable basis for prioritising which processes require immediate attention through either internal improvement or outsourcing.

- Cost analysis of internal departments in relation to service providers is an extremely challenging aspect of outsourcing. Unless the sourcing organisation and the service provider have standardised processes, it is not possible to derive fully objective cost comparisons. However, a key benefit of cost analysis is that it provides a mechanism for identifying how costs can be reduced via internal process redesign or outsourcing.

- Business improvement techniques such as workflow mapping are important in improving performance in outsourcing relationships. Workflow mapping can be employed to remove inefficiencies from processes both prior to outsourcing and during outsourcing arrangements.

Acknowledgements

The research team would like to thank CIMA for providing financial support for this research project. The research team would also like to acknowledge the support given by the financial services organisation that participated in the research. Valuable information and insights were provided by the management team on outsourcing and performance measurement in a real-world context.

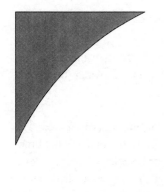

Chapter 1

Introduction

Outsourcing is increasingly being employed to achieve performance improvements across the entire business. However, many organisations have had mixed results with outsourcing. Indeed, many organisations have failed to achieve the desired benefits associated with outsourcing and experienced the consequences of outsourcing failure. This research project examines the issue of performance measurement in the outsourcing decision and has the following objectives:

■ To review the relevant literature on outsourcing, with particular emphasis on how companies benchmark internal performance with that of potential suppliers.

- To determine how a service organisation assesses the costs associated with the outsourcing decision.

- To determine how performance measures can be employed to evaluate the outsourcing decision and assess the performance of the service provider throughout the contract once a process is outsourced.

The research is positioned in the business process outsourcing (BPO) area. The analysis undertaken focused on performance measurement in the outsourcing process both at the corporate strategy and process level. Analysis at the process level is important as organisations increasingly outsource complex processes that extend across a range of business functions including finance, human resource management and information technology. The research was undertaken with a UK financial services organisation over a 4 year period. An action research methodology was applied to the research, which involved the research team engaging directly with the organisation during the evaluation and management phases of the outsourcing process. The research focused on a number of processes that this organisation had outsourced and examined how performance measurement considerations could be better integrated into the outsourcing process.

The book is structured as follows. An in-depth review of the literature in the area of outsourcing and performance measurement is presented. This review identifies a number of weaknesses in both the literature and practice. The next chapter includes an overview of an outsourcing framework, which was developed to overcome these weaknesses. In particular, this framework employs a number of tools and techniques that allows organisations to integrate performance measurement considerations into the outsourcing process. The framework provides guidelines on deciding whether outsourcing is appropriate, and if so, how the outsourcing process should be managed in order to improve performance. Case illustrations from the financial services organisation that participated in the research are introduced at various stages in order to illustrate this outsourcing framework in practice. An evaluation of the utility of the framework in practice is presented. Finally, in the concluding chapter management implications are presented.

Chapter 2

Literature Review

Outsourcing has increasingly become a vital tool for the implementation of business strategy in many organisations. Competition continues to increase and organisations are being continuously forced to find ways to improve business performance and to obtain competitive advantage. Increasingly, organisations are looking beyond the traditional boundaries of the firm to obtain performance improvement. The growing prevalence of outsourcing service providers is shaping the development of competitive strategies as well. The BPO phenomenon has grown as organisations have been transferring responsibility for entire functions such as human resource management, finance and information services to service providers – sometimes referred to as 'unbundling' (Hagel and Singer, 1999). According to Nelson Hall, the BPO tracking company, the global business process outsourcing market was worth $48.4 billion for the first three quarters of 2006, representing a rise of 34% from the same period in 2005 (Nelson Hall, 2006). Information technology and human resources are particular growth areas for outsourcing. Outsourcing has grown in reaction to the need for organisations to be more flexible and responsive to customer requirements. The outcome of increased outsourcing has been the restructuring of organisations from hierarchies performing the majority of business processes to more network-oriented structures working with specialist suppliers (McIvor, 2005). Gottfredson et al. (2005) suggested that competitive advantage from a capability perspective is no longer concerned with a company's ownership of capabilities but more exactly about its ability to control critical capabilities, whether owned or outsourced.

Outsourcing has become increasingly complex with both strategic and operational implications. In addition, there are many possible types of outsourcing arrangements, all of which redefine the boundaries of the firm, are dynamic in nature and subject to change over time. Therefore, performance measurement within the outsourcing process has become increasingly complex. Perhaps unsurprisingly, many firms lack a detailed understanding of outsourcing, particularly with regard to the potential benefits and risks. Outsourcing involves the sourcing of goods and services previously produced internally within an organisation from external suppliers. The term outsourcing can cover many areas, including the outsourcing of manufacturing as well as services. Outsourcing can involve the transfer of an entire business process to a supplier. Alternatively, outsourcing may lead to the transfer of some activities associated with the process whilst some are kept in-house. Outsourcing can also involve the transfer of both people and physical assets to the supplier. Organisations have always employed external product and service providers to carry out a range of business activities such as security, distribution, accounting and information technology. However, many organisations are increasingly outsourcing a wider range of activities and a greater level of the value associated with these activities. In effect, organisations are no longer outsourcing peripheral activities alone but extending the scope of outsourcing to encompass more critical activities that impact upon competitive position. Also, the recent movement of many service-related activities such as after-sales support and direct marketing offshore to developing economies has become increasingly prevalent. Outsourcing is not just a straightforward financial or purchasing decision. In many cases, outsourcing is a major strategic decision as organisations increasingly focus on a limited number of core competencies. Indeed, there is evidence to suggest that well-defined outsourcing strategies can enhance the overall strategy of the organisation (Gottfredson et al., 2005).

The evaluation and management of the outsourcing process involves a number of important elements. A starting point in the evaluation process involves analysing whether outsourcing a process is appropriate for the organisation. This involves considering issues such as the capability of the organisation in the process relative to competitors, the importance of the process to competitive advantage, the capability of suppliers to provide the process, the level of risk in the supply market, potential workforce resistance and the impact upon employee morale (McIvor, 2005). Where the decision to outsource has been made, a number of important issues have to be considered including supplier selection, contract negotiation and the transitioning of assets to the supplier. Also, significant attention should be given to managing the relationship with the supplier to ensure that outsourcing meets its intended objectives. The evaluation and management of the outsourcing process has become increasingly complex. For example, contracts are more complex as agreements become more sophisticated in terms of measurement procedures, the financial management of transferred assets and the inclusion of clauses associated with bringing the process back in-house (Quelin and Duhamel, 2003). Also, the presence of political influences on the decision-making process, such as the vested interests of the functions under scrutiny to keep the relevant activities in-house, can prevent the choice of the most appropriate sourcing option for the organisation. The strategic nature of the decision means that it not only involves input from operational management, but also from senior management. Considerable care and effort has to be given to evaluating and managing the outsourcing process. Outsourcing decisions are extremely costly and difficult to reverse. For example, in a study of outsourcing, Barthelemy and Geyer (2000) found that in the event of outsourcing not meeting its intended objectives, it can take an average of 8–9 months to switch to another service provider or bring the process back in-house at the end of the contract.

2.1 The development of outsourcing

Outsourcing has become a vital ingredient of corporate restructuring initiatives. Much of the early literature and studies on outsourcing have focused on manufacturing (Higgins, 1955; Culliton, 1956). Historically, manufacturing outsourcing – often referred to as the make-or-buy decision – has been more prevalent. In the 1980s and 1990s a considerable amount of attention was given to manufacturing outsourcing and the implications for the long-term competitiveness of both organisations and economies (Bettis et al., 1992; Venkatesan, 1992; Welch and Nayak, 1992). Outsourcing in manufacturing became very prominent in the 1980s, in part as a result of the rise of 'lean production', a paradigm developed from analysis of Japanese production and supply systems (Womack et al., 1990). Outsourcing in this context involved the development of longer-term supplier relationships, which were characterised by collaboration and joint problem solving in a range of areas. Adopting collaborative supplier relationships were viewed as means of reducing the risks associated with outsourcing in cases where the requirements of the buyer were not standardised and the transaction involved frequent changes.

More recently, a similar process of outsourcing has been occurring in the area of business services (Sako, 2006; McIvor, 2007). For example, an insurance company can now outsource its claims handling process to a service provider that manages the contact centre and related back-office infrastructure. Business services are services that are provided to other businesses, rather than directly to the public (Abramovsky et al., 2004). Examples of business services include computer services, professional services (legal, accountancy, market research, technical, engineering, advertising, human resources and consultancy), research and development (R&D), recruitment agencies and call centres. Between 1984 and 2001 the growth in the business services sector accounted for around one-third of the total output growth in the UK economy. Outsourcing and offshoring in this area has grown as the services sector has developed. There are a number of drivers of the trend towards outsourcing and offshoring.

2.1.1 DEVELOPMENTS IN INFORMATION AND COMMUNICATION TECHNOLOGIES

The advent of relatively cheap and reliable telecommunications and information technology has facilitated the trend towards outsourcing. The increasing importance of innovative ICTs for economies and societies has been attracting considerable attention both from academia and practitioners. In the last number of decades ICTs have deeply affected the way business is performed and the way in which organisations compete (Porter, 2001). Developments in ICTs have enabled organisations to transfer responsibility for processes to service providers both locally and offshore. Using the analogy of Evans and Wurster (1999), it is now possible for organisations to separate the information element from the physical elements in service processes. Processes such as market research, customer service and product support are highly information intensive and can be sourced from service providers both locally and offshore. For example, offshore service providers can now offer IT-enabled customer support processes to customers anywhere in the world regardless of their physical location. Separating the information element from the physical element of business processes allows an organisation to fundamentally re-think and re-engineer its operations in ways that reduce costs and enhance value for their customers (Youngdahl and Ramaswamy, 2007).

2.1.2 BUSINESS PROCESS PERSPECTIVE

The business process view championed by Hammer and Davenport and consultancy firms such as Accenture and Genpact has had a major influence on how organisations view their operations and outsource business processes. Process management is a structured approach to performance improvement that focuses on the disciplined design and careful execution of an organisation's end-to-end business processes (Hammer, 2002). Hammer defines a business process as an organised group of related processes that work together to create value for customers. Previously, organisations developed their own processes such as order fulfilment, customer support and order processing, which were company and location specific. These processes were constructed to meet the idiosyncrasies of individual organisations. However, as a result of business process improvement, information technology implementations and total quality management (TQM) initiatives organisations have embarked upon mapping processes and improving process performance across the entire business. A major element of these initiatives has involved standardising and outsourcing processes to specialist service providers (Davenport, 2005). Shared services arrangements in outsourcing have arisen as a result of the standardisation and centralisation of processes associated with business functions such as information technology, human resources, finance and accounting and R&D. Shared services arrangements involve the centralising of processes at a single location where the geographically dispersed units of an organisation share the services centrally rather than have all the services provided locally (Metters and Verma, 2007).

2.1.3 GLOBALISATION

Over the last number of years the external business environment has become increasingly global for many industries. Many organisations are now competing on a global basis. Regional agreements such as the North American Free Trade Agreement (NAFTA) between the USA, Canada and Mexico, and the development of the European market with a single currency have facilitated the development of trade on a global basis. This trend has led organisations to expand the geographical scope of their business operations in terms of the markets they serve and the production locations for the creation of their products and services. These changes have presented organisations with significant opportunities. For example, companies have been in a position to achieve greater economies of scale, share investments in R&D and marketing across their various markets, and access lower cost labour sources for both the manufacture of their products and delivery of their services. Furthermore, countries such as India and Ireland have proactively developed their competitiveness and encouraged large multinational firms to locate much of their service requirements to their shores (Kripalani and Engardio, 2003). These countries have developed their attractiveness through investments in their telecommunications infrastructure, low corporation taxes, favourable business legislation, competitive labour costs and a strong emphasis on education.

2.1.4 PUBLIC SECTOR REFORMS

The trend towards increased outsourcing has also been influenced by wide-ranging reforms occurring in public sector organisations in many countries (McIvor, 2005). For example, successive governments in the USA and UK have pursued radical public sector reforms which have placed the use of competitive market mechanisms at the heart of these reforms. Proponents of this philosophy argue that assets and processes should be transferred from the public sector to the private sector in order to improve performance. Also, these proponents argue that the public sector should aspire to levels of performance attained in the private sector. The constant drive for cost reduction and the efficient use of resources forced many public sector organisations to consider reducing the scale of government departments and public services. This trend towards radically changing the large hierarchical nature of public sector organisations with more responsive customer-oriented network structures is in common with the changes occurring in many commercial organisations. However, these developments in the public sector have been very controversial. For example, the high level of unionisation in the public sector has hindered the freedom with which governments can pursue such reforms.

2.2 The benefits of outsourcing

2.2.1 COST REDUCTION

Organisations can achieve considerable cost reductions through outsourcing strategies. Outsourcing enables the outsourcing organisation to benefit from supplier cost advantages such as economies of scale, experience and location (TPI, 2007). Suppliers may take on investment and development costs while sharing these risks among many customers and thereby reducing supplier costs for all customers. For example, in the financial services industry many banks have outsourced high-volume transaction processing functions such as electronic payments and processing of cheques to service providers with greater economies of scale in order to reduce the cost of each transaction (Lancellotti et al., 2003). Furthermore, by gradually outsourcing processes the customer can reduce risks by converting its fixed costs into variable costs. In times of adverse business conditions service providers will then have to deal with the problem of excess capacity. However, service providers should be better able to cope with demand fluctuations through economies of scale and have more scope for alternative sources for excess capacity.

2.2.2 PERFORMANCE IMPROVEMENT

Service providers can often achieve much higher levels of performance in certain processes than can be achieved internally by the outsourcing organisation. This performance advantage is based not only on reduced costs. Specialist suppliers can often provide higher levels of service quality than those of internal functions within the outsourcing organisation (Sako, 2006). The performance improvements that service providers can deliver has given rise to terms such as transactional and transformational outsourcing (Linder, 2004). Transactional outsourcing involves the service provider delivering process efficiencies and process improvement. Alternatively, transformational outsourcing involves the service provider delivering business and process transformation (Mani et al., 2006). The outsourced process shares inter-dependencies with other business processes, is complex and is strategically important to the customer organisation.

2.2.3 FLEXIBILITY

In the past, organisations attempted to control the majority of business processes internally on the assumption that controlling supply eliminates the possibility of short-run service disruptions or demand imbalances in its customer markets (Shi, 2007). However, such a strategy is both inflexible and inherently fraught with risks. Owing to issues such as cost pressures, rapid changes in technology and increasingly sophisticated consumers, it is very difficult for organisations to control and excel at all the processes that create competitive advantage. Outsourcing can provide an organisation with greater flexibility, especially in the sourcing of rapidly developing new technologies or fashion goods. Specialist suppliers can provide greater responsiveness through new technologies than large vertically integrated organisations.

2.2.4 SPECIALISATION

Outsourcing can allow an organisation to concentrate on areas of the business that drive competitive advantage and outsource peripheral processes enabling it to leverage the specialist skills of service providers. For example, Quinn (1999) argues that specialists in supply markets can develop greater knowledge depth, invest more in software and training systems, be more efficient and therefore offer higher salaries and attract more highly trained people than can the individual staff of all but a few integrated companies. These advantages can generate enough value to deliver a better service at a lower cost to the customer, whilst allowing the supplier to make a profit. Specialisation can also allow an organisation to gain a competitive advantage in its industry (Mani et al., 2006). For example, companies such as UPS, Solectron and Hewitt Associates have transformed their core functions into entirely new industries. Also, specialisation can have a positive impact upon career development opportunities for employees in specialist service providers. For example, in the case of employees in specialist functions such as information technology in large diverse organisations, the scope for career progression is normally limited to within a single function. However, there is evidence to show that when the same employees are transferred to a specialist organisation, there are enhanced career and training opportunities. For example, Kessler et al. (1999) have found in a study of outsourcing in local government that employees were much more positive about career development opportunities after being transferred to the service provider.

2.2.5 ACCESS TO INNOVATION

Many organisations are reluctant to outsource because they fear they may lose the capability for innovation in the future. However, in many supply markets there exists significant opportunities to leverage the capabilities of service providers into the services of the customer organisation. Rather than attempt to replicate the capabilities of service providers, it is much more prudent to use outsourcing to fully exploit the service providers' investments, innovations and specialist capabilities. Tesco, in its efforts to offer retail telecommunications services has outsourced the entire operation to a number of service providers including Cable and Wireless for the telecommunications service, Servista for billing support and Vertex Customer Management for customer service (Nairn, 2003). Each of these service providers is specialising in its own area of expertise whilst Tesco is enhancing its brand as a retail service provider.

2.3 The risks of outsourcing

2.3.1 COST INCREASES

There is evidence to suggest that when organisations outsource to achieve cost reductions, costs do not decrease as expected and in some cases can increase (Kern et al., 2002; Davison, 2004). When organisations outsource to achieve cost reductions, there is normally an early anticipation of cash benefits and long-term cost savings. However, many organisations fail to account for future costs and in particular that of managing the outsourcing process – sometimes referred to as the hidden costs of outsourcing (Barthelemy, 2001). There is a tendency to under-estimate the management resources and time that have to be invested in outsourcing. Some organisations fail to realise that resources have to be invested in managing the relationship with the service provider, which is particularly important in the case of critical business processes. Many organisations assume that labour arbitrage will deliver cost savings comparable with worker-to-worker substitution without consideration of the hidden costs of outsourcing (Shi, 2007). For example, outsourced workers absorbed elsewhere inside the customer organisation can dissipate the anticipated costs savings. In addition, extra project management resources allocated to managing the outsourcing arrangement will add to the overall costs. In many cases organisations outsource in order to effect improvements in certain parts of the business which have been causing problems. However, it is erroneous to assume that once the process is outsourced, the problem will disappear. For example, poor performance internally may have been due to weak management. It is often the case that the person previously responsible for managing the process internally is responsible for managing the external service provider. This problem is further exacerbated if the outsourcing process has involved the transfer of staff from the outsourcing organisation to the service provider. Therefore, it is important to determine why the process is being outsourced in the first place. Also, when an organisation outsources it may not identify certain aspects of the process that are provided internally, which can include issues such as employee goodwill or involvement of employees from other parts of the organisation. With such aspects being omitted from the contractual agreement, the service provider may add on extra charges for these services.

2.3.2   SUPPLY MARKET RISK

Organisations can encounter significant risks when they use service providers for processes that they have performed internally in the past. Over dependency on a particular service provider can lead to significant risks in terms of cost, quality and service provider failure (Caldwell, 2002). For example, service providers may fail to achieve the necessary quality standards demanded by the outsourcing organisation. Therefore, an organisation may decide to keep a process in-house in order to guarantee quality and reliability of supply. In relation to the supply market, it is crucial for the outsourcing company to monitor changes in the supply market. When a company chooses to outsource it may do so on the basis of the presence of competition amongst a number of service providers in the supply market. However, many organisations fail to monitor changes in the supply market and their impact upon the outsourcing process. For example, the balance of power may shift towards the supply market if there has been consolidation amongst a number of smaller service providers into a few large service providers. Such a situation may arise if the company undertakes outsourcing with limited experience of managing a supplier relationship and is dealing with astute service providers. Public sector organisations have had difficulties with monitoring and managing public sector contracts due a lack of the requisite skills and experience (McIvor, 2005). Many organisations fail to recognise that managing an external service provider requires a different set of skills than those associated with managing an internal department. Service providers in outsourcing markets are extremely adept at exploiting any naiveté on the part of the outsourcing organisation in areas such as contract negotiation and relationship management. For example, Barthelemy (2003) has found that outsourcing failure is often a result of poorly drafted contracts that lack precision (i.e. additional fees were paid for basic services), flexibility (i.e. fixed fees had been set when business was booming) and completeness (i.e. huge penalties involved with switching vendors).

2.3.3 Loss of Skills

Outsourcing can lead to the loss of critical skills and the potential for innovation in the future (Kern et al., 2002). In the long term, an organisation needs to maintain innovative capacity in a number of key processes in order to exploit new opportunities in its respective customer markets. If an organisation has outsourced a number of critical processes its ability to innovate may be severely diminished. Innovation requires slack resources, organic and fluid organisational processes and experimental competencies – all attributes that outside supply does not guarantee (Earl, 1996). These risks can become more pronounced when the objectives of the outsourcing company and the service provider are conflicting. For example, the customer organisation may decide to establish a short-term contract with a service provider in order to obtain the lowest price and keep the supplier in a weak position. However, this will seriously undermine any incentive for the supplier to pass on any of the benefits associated with innovation to the customer organisation. Service providers can also become competitors in the future once they obtain the requisite knowledge and skills to deliver the entire service requirements of which the outsourced process is a significant element (Mani et al., 2006).

2.3.4 Organisational Change Implications

Outsourcing has significant social implications for an organisation (McIvor, 2005). The social implications of outsourcing are often ignored in favour of the need to reduce costs. However, the effective management of the social implications is crucial as employees view outsourcing as a denigration of their performance, which can often lead to industrial action. Outsourcing can lead to the redeployment of staff within the outsourcing organisation or the transfer of staff to the service provider. The demands associated with outsourcing transcend organisational boundaries, and therefore, the approach to managing the change process must ensure that complementary processes and behaviours are exhibited within and between organisations. However, organisations have had extreme difficulties with embracing and effectively managing the change process required (McIvor and McHugh, 2002). For example, a new focus on quality and customer relationships necessitates changes in policies, cultural values, work procedures and processes, relationship between departments and interactions between buyers and suppliers. Organisations often ignore the fact that successful outsourcing is heavily dependent upon the attitudes and commitment of their workforce. Outsourcing has a negative impact upon the job security and loyalty of employees even when they retain their positions in the outsourcing organisation (Barthelemy, 2003). The perspectives and responses of employees at all levels and positions have a significant impact on the successful implementation of strategic change processes. For example, key employees should be retained and motivated, which involves identifying employees with important process knowledge. Furthermore, given the strategic nature of the decision to outsource, culture change is vital. However, effecting culture change is an enormous task. Frequently, organisations fail to engage in a process whereby time, money and efforts are invested in bringing about a change in culture, structure and reward systems (Boddy et al., 1998). The strategy of organisations tends to focus on content issues such as the achievement of efficiencies, while ignoring the process of how to achieve the efficiencies.

2.4 Key motivations for outsourcing

2.4.1 COST EFFICIENCIES

Insinga and Werle (2000) have argued that organisations are increasingly faced with pressures to deliver more with fewer resources. They proposed that the primary goal of outsourcing is to enhance competitiveness by reducing capital investment commitments to increase the ability to adjust quickly to a changing environment. Such a motivation is linked to the need for technology and may result in either a business process outsourcing/full service provision arrangement or in a collaborative co-sourcing arrangement depending on the importance of the technology to competitive advantage. Insinga and Werle (2000), whilst considering outsourcing to be a strategic decision, viewed it primarily as a means of reducing costs. Whilst outsourcing has moved on from being merely a cost reduction tool, the achievement of cost efficiencies and cost control still remain the primary objectives of outsourcing (Lancellotti et al., 2003; Quelin and Duhamel, 2003; Burdon and Bhalla, 2005). A comprehensive survey of outsourcing in 2003 in the European banking industry by McKinsey, in collaboration with IBM and the EFMA, found that 44% of banks considered efficiency gains as the primary or even sole outsourcing objective (Lancellotti et al., 2003). The desired cost savings in both these industries was consistent at between 10% and 20%. It is important to position the possible cost savings from outsourcing against other internal improvement techniques. Bryce and Usseem (1998) reported that business process reengineering could create cost savings of over 50% whilst in manufacturing industries the introduction of lean production can generate 50% cost reductions. Average cost savings of 15% through outsourcing initiatives are modest by comparison.

2.4.2 FOCUSING ON CORE COMPETENCIES

Whilst Harland et al. (2005) acknowledged the strategy of focusing on organisational core competencies to Prahalad and Hamel (1990), they suggested that the antecedent of this view dates back to the late 1960s; an organisation can benefit from concentrating on a small number of manageable tasks in which it becomes excellent (Skinner, 1969). Core competency strategies have produced a major motivation for outsourcing. Such strategies became popular in manufacturing and consumer packaged goods industries in the late 1980s and early 1990s. This was a period of relatively low economic growth and high unemployment rates. Several industries had become capital intensive rather than labour intensive and large capital investments were necessary to generate improvements in labour productivity and process capabilities (De Kok and Graves, 2006). Focusing on core competencies meant the outsourcing of non-core competencies. This reduced the fixed cost burden on these firms virtually instantaneously and produced dramatic effects on their return on investment (ROI) measures and related performance indicators. De Kok and Graves (2006) highlighted that outsourcing produced multinational brand-owners focussing on marketing, R&D and procurement and multinational 'service companies' focussing on manufacturing and logistics. Whilst there may not be the capital investment parallel in an industry like financial services, competition has meant that revenue for financial services organisations has become much more dependent on achieving aggressive sales growth. Consequently, there has been a desire to utilise experienced staff much more on selling than on transaction processing and administration.

2.4.3 ENHANCED RELIABILITY AND QUALITY

While cost efficiencies may be a principle objective of outsourcing; enhanced reliability and quality and access to best practice (Bryce and Usseem, 1998; Quelin and Duhamel, 2003; Burdon and Bhalla, 2005) are additional motives. Bryce and Usseem (1998) reported that the organisations most likely to engage in outsourcing initiatives were high cost producers and firms that are under-performing. This indicates that the motivations are both cost related and focused on improving capabilities. This view is supported by Teng et al. (1995) who suggested that the outsourcing of information services might be strategically inevitable if performance began to slide in a competitive and technologically complex environment. Teng et al. (1995) proposed that a firm's inclination to outsource was often related to discrepancies in either actual or desired levels of performance in the areas of cost effectiveness or quality. Much of the extant literature confirms that motivations for outsourcing are strategic (Insinga and Werle, 2000; Franceschini et al., 2003; Quelin and Duhamel, 2003; Lacity et al., 2004; Harland et al., 2005; McIvor, 2005; Espino-Rodriguez and Padron-Robaina, 2006; Holcomb and Hitt, 2007). Bryce and Usseem (1998) cited three principle ways that outsourcing could contribute to strategic advantage: by enabling a firm to access expertise not available in-house; provide a complementary resource or capability that produces synergistic benefits when combined with internal capabilities;

provide a way to learn the specialised skills of the outsourcing provider. These are the types of strategic benefits being sought when an organisation chooses to engage in a strategic outsourcing arrangement.

2.5   Types of outsourcing arrangements

An outsourcing initiative transfers responsibility for the ongoing management and execution of a business activity, process or functional area to an external provider with the objective of improved performance. It is important to stress that the external provider may be owned by the outsourcing firm, for example in the case of the creation of a spin-off company. It is a common misconception that outsourcing ventures necessitate the transfer of ownership of a process or function entirely to an external service provider. From the service provider's perspective, business processes and functions are described as horizontal or vertical; horizontal processes are cross-industry whilst vertical processes are industry specific. Gottfredson et al. (2005) has proposed that capability sourcing will become the mechanism for organisational redesign. The outsourcing decision is made no less complex by the fact that the term outsourcing means different things to different people. Gilley and Rasheed (2000) acknowledged this uncertainty and attempted to provide a definitive explanation of outsourcing. They argued that outsourcing represents the fundamental decision to reject the internalisation of a process and can take two different forms: substitution of external purchases for internal processes or abstention of possible internal processes that could have been established in favour of external provision. Such a narrow definition has not been embraced by outsourcing scholars or practitioners. Espino-Rodriguez and Padron-Robaina (2006) stated that the academic outsourcing literature defines the outsourcing phenomenon in ways that highlight the scholar's specific research focus as summarised in Table 2.1.

There is a vast array of terms used in the outsourcing literature and there appears to be little convergence of the terminology used between academia and practice. This can only serve to perpetuate confusion surrounding the subject. However, there are a number of configurations to manage outsourcing arrangements both locally and offshore. Using the dimensions of level of ownership and location, a typology of outsourcing and offshore arrangements can be created as shown in Figure 2.1. Each of these arrangements is now discussed.

2.5.1   LOCAL IN-HOUSE SOURCING

This occurs when an organisation sources services internally from business functions such as human resources, information technology and finance and accounting.

Table 2.1 A summary of outsourcing definitions

Focus of outsourcing definition	References
Outsourcing entails a stable long-term collaboration agreement.	Mol et al. (2005), Quelin and Duhamel (2003), McIvor (2000)
Non-strategic processes are most suitable for outsourcing.	Casani et al. (1996), Lei and Hitt (1995), Quinn and Hilmer (1994)
A contract is the means by which the planning, responsibility, knowledge, and administration of processes is transferred to an external party.	McCarthy and Anagnostou (2004), Blumberg (1998)
Outsourcing can be used to obtain key capabilities to supplement existing capabilities.	Holcomb and Hitt (2007)

Source: Adapted from Espino-Rodriguez and Padron Robaina (2006).

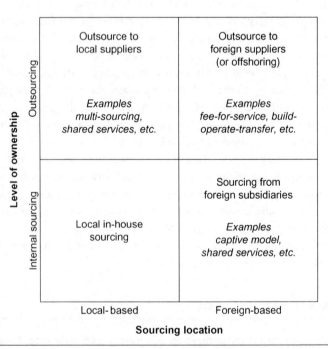

Figure 2.1 A typology of sourcing configurations.

2.5.2 OUTSOURCING TO LOCAL SERVICE PROVIDERS

This option involves an organisation sourcing services from service providers within its national boundaries. There are a number of configurations organisations employed for local outsourcing. Robinson and Kalakota (2004) have found that organisations are increasingly utilising multi-sourcing instead of moving directly to totally externally owned outsourcing arrangements. Multi-sourcing integrates in-house service provision with outsourced methods; either 'out-tasking' some of the steps in a process or total business process outsourcing. Robinson and Kalakota (2004) argued that out-tasking is often a practical way of exploring the potential benefits of total outsourcing without the risks of total dependency. Organisations are also using local service providers to manage shared service arrangements rather than using internal sources.

2.5.3 SOURCING FROM FOREIGN SUBSIDIARIES

This arrangement involves an organisation establishing and managing a subsidiary in a foreign location to avail of local skills and lower labour costs. A common model associated with this arrangement is the captive model. With the captive model, the customer builds, owns, staffs and operates the offshore facility (Rottman and Lacity, 2004). The captive model offers a high level of control through ownership but also carries high levels of risk due to the inflexibility associated with ownership. Global shared service arrangements are often established via the captive model. For example, American Express consolidated more than 46 transaction processing sites in 3 shared service centres located in the USA, UK and India (Robinson and Kalakota, 2004). The captive model allowed American Express to reduce its overall costs, primarily as a result of lower labour costs in India, and transferring work amongst regional service centres to provide capacity flexibility and serve customers on a global basis 24 hours per day.

2.5.4 OUTSOURCING TO FOREIGN SERVICE PROVIDERS

This arrangement involves sourcing services from an independent service provider in foreign locations – often referred to as offshoring. Again, there are a number of models employed by organisations which are largely influenced by the level of control required. Organisations can use external service providers on a contractual basis. For example, this is the case with fee-for-service offshore outsourcing in areas such as software development and customer contact where the customer signs a contract with an offshore service provider who owns its own facility and employs its own staff. This is the most popular offshore outsourcing model as it offers the lowest level of risk (Rottman and Lacity, 2004). Another common model in offshore outsourcing is the joint venture where the customer and the supplier share ownership in the facility.

Organisations often chose a joint venture over the captive model because they want to sacrifice control in exchange for the supplier taking on most of the risk. The build-operate-transfer (BOT) model is often associated with the joint venture model. This model provides an opportunity to leverage the capabilities of a service provider to establish offshore operations and then transfer the operations to the full control of the customer after an agreed period of time. The BOT model has become increasingly prevalent in many industries where distinctive capabilities are built around unique knowledge bases such as design and engineering (Youngdahl et al., 2007).

2.6 Outsourcing and performance measurement

The increasing sophistication of outsourcing strategies makes performance measurement a complex issue. Performance measures are needed in an outsourcing context to assess whether or not outsourcing is helping to achieve the strategic objectives of the business. Much of the literature agrees that competitive priorities are concerned with issues of quality, cost, delivery and flexibility (Shin et al., 2000; Krause et al., 2001; Slack and Lewis, 2002). In addition, the need to link performance measurement with competitive strategy has been identified using four distinct performance dimensions and indicators of cost/productivity, time, flexibility and quality (De Toni and Tonchia, 2001). The critical success factor (CSF) method is a useful technique for linking competitive strategy and outsourcing with performance. CSFs represent those areas of the organisation that management needs to focus on to create high levels of performance. Rockart (1979) was the first to define the concept of CSFs as the limited numbers of areas in which results, if they are satisfactory, will ensure competitive performance for the organisation. The CSF approach is an accepted top-down methodology to assist business strategy development. Examples of CSFs include the development of a global sales network, superior new product development and the development of a best-in-class supply base. Between four and eight CSFs can be identified as crucial to the performance of most organisations. The sources of CSFs will be influenced by a number of factors including industry characteristics, stage of the industry value chain and the needs of customers groups.

Once CSFs have been determined, they can be used as a basis for determining the importance level of processes for outsourcing evaluation. The CSFs should translate into a number of critical processes that create value for the organisation. The first step in this analysis involves determining how specific processes contribute to the achievement of the CSFs. For example, a CSF such as 'the provision of innovative new services' needs to be clearly defined in terms of what it exactly means. In effect, the organisation is identifying what has to be done in order to meet the CSFs that are central to its current and future success. Once the CSFs have been determined, it is also important to consider how they can be integrated into the performance measurement system.

An important technique for linking CSFs with performance is benchmarking. Prior to outsourcing, organisations must have an understanding of the key measures that indicate performance in a process relative to suppliers or competitors. As well as considering costs, the relative performance along a number of other dimensions such as quality, flexibility and service should be considered. The purpose of benchmarking comparisons is to enable companies to determine where and how performance can be improved. It is concerned with searching for and implementing best practice and performance improvement so that the organisation can understand and incorporate process or product innovations that have been successful in other contexts. Benchmarking should not be just focused on measuring outcomes but should be equally concerned with the processes employed to produce the outcomes (Wisniewski, 2001). Employing benchmarking in outsourcing allows an organisation to align operational processes at the lower level with the overall business strategy of the organisation. Furthermore, benchmarking assists organisations in optimising their capability to meet the needs of customers by ensuring that processes are more superior, consistent and effective than competitors. Therefore, it can be used as a basis for building competitive advantage. A critical part of benchmarking is the selection and manipulation of metrics to represent the performance of the process under analysis. Table 2.2 shows a sample of potential performance metrics for use in the finance and accounting function.

Table 2.2 Potential metrics for finance and accounting

Function	Performance dimension	Specific measures
Finance and Accounting	Cost effectiveness	Cost per invoice
		Cost per remittance
	Staff productivity	Invoices processed per accounts payable full time equivalent (FTE)
		Remittances processed per accounts receivable FTE
	Process efficiency	Error exception rate
		Payroll processing error rate
		Invoice processing rate
	Cycle time	Average time to process an invoice
		Days sales outstanding

Source: Adapted from Skogstad (2004).

There are different classifications of benchmarking:

• *Strategic benchmarking – This is used to compare organisational structures and management practices and business strategies. Organisations may have similar approaches or initiatives to achieve strategic objectives that are comparable.*

• *Process benchmarking – This is particularly valuable in an outsourcing context and is used to compare operations, work practices and business processes. Process benchmarking involves developing a detailed understanding of how a particular process is carried out and comparing it to how it is carried out and measuring it against performance levels in that process with other organisations.*

• *Product benchmarking – This is used to compare products and/or services. This is similar to reverse product engineering that focuses on the analysis of specific components and functions of the products of competitors. Also, reverse engineering can act as a starting point for process benchmarking. For example, the analysis can be extended to include an examination of the processes that underpin the products of competitors.*

(Carpinetti and de Melo 2002)

As well as considering performance prior to outsourcing, performance measurement is an important element of managing the relationship with the service provider. During the relationship, performance targets have been considered to be a control mechanism with varying degrees of importance depending on the type of outsourcing arrangement (Langfield-Smith and Smith, 2003). They have argued that rigid performance targets were most important in outsourcing arrangements where the provider was chosen due to their capabilities. Such outsourcing relationships tend to have moderate levels of dependency, but high levels of emphasis on measuring outputs. There is also a growing body of literature (Klaas et al., 2001) that suggests that either outsourcing or in-house provision will not have a direct impact by itself on performance. Performance outcomes are likely to be affected by particular factors such as the management of the outsourcing relationship by the outsourcing organisation. It has been suggested that a firm may gain control over an outsourced function through ongoing monitoring of work performance alongside monitoring aspects of the relationship (McFarlan and Nolan, 1995). They suggested that this might be achieved by using performance measurements and benchmark metrics focusing on market outcomes, for example customer satisfaction, financial outcomes, for example cost figures, or operational areas such as delivery responsiveness and product quality. McFarlan and Nolan (1995) advocated that performance measurements could be either included within the contract or negotiated later on.

A key aspect of the outsourcing contract in relation to performance management is the service level agreement (SLA). The SLA is an agreement between the customer and the supplier that quantifies the service levels required by the customer (Larson, 1998). The SLA should describe the types, scope and nature of all the services required, the times when these services should be available and the level of performance required. Clearly defined services and service levels are critical elements of an outsourcing contract. Larson (1998) argues that the key to successful outsourcing involves defining services and service levels that can be measured and managed; can be audited; can be provided at an economic price; and give maximum value to the users of the services. The SLA should also allow the buying organisation to measure the performance of the supplier through a number of mechanisms including regular progress meetings, inspection procedures, etc.

2.7   Management accounting and outsourcing

Management accounting techniques have had an influence on the trend towards outsourcing. Indeed, there is a considerable history of accounting problems associated with asset financing via non-conventional funding, particularly in the private sector. Leasing was one method adopted by 'creative accountants' in the 1980s as a means of recording assets and related liabilities 'off balance sheet', thereby circumventing budget restrictions. Standard Statement of Accounting Practice (SSAP) 21 (ASC, 1984) was published to prevent this by ensuring that finance leases be capitalised and their associated finance recorded as liabilities in the lessee's (i.e. the user's) financial statements. This would ensure that the party having control over the asset would have to place that asset in its own books and not in the books of the legal owner of the asset. This would result in the substance of a transaction prevailing over its legal form. In practice, the standard was not particularly successful as lessees manipulated the SSAP, mainly by the adoption of larger than realistic residual values for assets (Loveday, 1991), and by the inclusion of separate maintenance payments to give the impression that the lessor retained control over those assets. Work is still ongoing by accounting regulators to try and do away with the distinction between operating leases (categorised as expenditure) and finance leases (categorised as an asset), which is often exploited, and make all leasing arrangements finance leases.

In 1994 the Accounting Standards Board (ASB) issued Financial Reporting Standard (FRS) 5, which ensured that the concept of substance over form had been developed into an accounting standard in its own right (ASB, 1994). However, the launch of the Private Finance Initiative (PFI) in 1992 gave rise to further uncertainties as to the correct accounting treatment of specific assets. Under PFI, a private sector consortium undertakes to design, build, finance and operate a major public sector infrastructure asset such as a prison or hospital. Concerns that the resulting asset, and its associated liability, were incorrectly appearing on the private sector's balance sheet led to the issuing of an application note to FRS 5 on the topic of PFI which reinforced the main principle, that is that substance should take precedence over a transaction's legal form (ASB, 1998). In order to determine who, in essence, accounts for an asset in a contract, it is essential to identify which party has access to the benefits arising from the property and exposure to the risks emanating from that property.

Outsourcing circumvents a number of the aforementioned problems. The contractor is exposed to most of the risks and, in the majority of cases, is using its own assets. Therefore, the substance over form question does not arise; the contractor accounts for its own assets and the outsourcing company pays for the service as and when it is provided. However, a ruling by the International Accounting Standards Board (IASB) may affect the accounting treatment of outsourcing deals [see IASB (2004) for details of International Financial Reporting Interpretations Committee (IFRIC) 4]. Outsourcing contracts, especially those involving situations where the vendor owns assets such as servers, desktops and printers may be considered as leases under these new rules. Outsourcing customers are likely to find that these new rulings have a significant impact on their balance sheets, depreciation schedules and, potentially, even their earnings. Rather than treating outsourcing contracts as purely services agreements and therefore expensing the cost, companies may discover that they have to capitalise a portion of these contracts, depending on the asset-related services in their agreements. The effect on the balance sheet could be substantial.

2.7.1 ECONOMIC VALUE ADDED

Economic value added is generally known as EVA® and is a registered trademark of Stern Stewart & Co. It was created as a reaction to both the lack of clarity and rigorousness of measures such as ROI (Stewart, 1991). The full application of the method calls for 160 separate accounting adjustments. Not surprisingly, therefore, many companies see only some of these as necessary, so calculate a somewhat simplified EVA. Notwithstanding, some of its main features are as follows:

• *Some generally accepted accounting principle (GAAP) treatments of expenses and assets are altered: for example R&D costs (which are commonly expensed as incurred) are capitalised and then amortised over their useful life; long-term lease payments (capitalised under GAAP) revert to being expenses (with the related depreciation eliminated); and any increase in the provision for bad debts is eliminated.*

• *These adjustments give rise to the EVA version of pre-tax operating income, from which taxes (but not interest expense) are deducted. The figure used for tax is the cash tax payment that will be made on the basis of the earnings for the year; therefore any adjustment for deferred tax disappears.*

• *With regard to asset valuation, the book value of most of the assets shown on the balance sheet is used (i.e. historic cost, less accumulated depreciation), inventories are shown at market value, and also added are the provision for bad debts and the capitalised R&D costs. The asset value is reduced by the amount of the current liabilities, on the basis that these (predominantly trade payables) are provided free of interest.*

• *The company's weighted average cost of capital is used as the relevant interest rate. That is, the cost of equity, multiplied by the proportion of equity in the capital structure, plus the after-tax cost of debt, multiplied by the proportion of debt in the capital structure.*

(Adapted from Parkinson, 2004)

It is this latter point that makes outsourcing an attractive proposition to organisations. By reducing the amount of capital assets on their books (e.g. plant and equipment, IT systems and even buildings), a company also reduces the amount of liabilities on the balance sheet, thereby reducing the cost of capital and improving its EVA. Stern Stewart (2000) felt that outsourcing is a key strategic component in capital management. However, it felt that with regard to EVA, outsourcing was not only used to reduce capital costs but also to make capital variable and to reduce overall costs, both operating (e.g. personnel, energy) and capital.

2.8   Problems with the outsourcing process

Although the trend towards outsourcing has increased in recent years, many organisations have experienced considerable difficulties with achieving their desired objectives. Gottfredson et al. (2005) have found that 82% of large firms in Europe, Asia and North America have engaged in some type of outsourcing arrangement. However, almost half of these firms have failed to meet their initial outsourcing expectations. In fact, it has been argued that outsourcing decisions are made most frequently by default with little consideration for the long-run competitiveness of the organisation. Although there are a number outsourcing frameworks, few companies have taken a strategic view of outsourcing decisions, with many companies still deciding to outsource based upon short-term cost-reduction motives (Davison, 2004; McIvor, 2005). Furthermore, Aron and Singh (2005) have found that companies are spending insufficient time on evaluating which processes that they should and should not outsource. An outline of the major limitations of practice and existing literature in the area of outsourcing is now presented.

2.8.1 No Formal Outsourcing Process

Many organisations have no structured basis for evaluating the outsourcing decision and, in particular, do not place the decision in a strategic context. A recent survey by Deloitte Consulting (2005) has found that 70% of respondents had negative
experiences of outsourcing. Rather than achieve their outsourcing objectives, this
survey found that many organisations are still underestimating the costs and complexities of implementing outsourcing arrangements. The choice of which parts of
the business to outsource is made by ascertaining what will save most on overhead
costs, rather than on what makes the most long-term business sense. This can create
a situation in which the organisation is outsourcing processes that are a source of
competitive advantage. Organisations are failing to consider issues such as:

- Should the organisation strive to maintain and build its capability in a particular
  process or turn to the best-in-class service provider?
- Does the necessary capacity exist within the organisation to provide the process?
- Do the internal capabilities of the organisation in a particular process lag behind
  potential suppliers?
- If there is a performance disparity between sourcing organisation and service
  provider, how much resource is required internally to match the capabilities of
  the external service providers?

2.8.2 Misapplication of the Core Competence Concept

The use of the core competence approach has dominated the approaches to outsourcing by practitioners. The core competence concept has evolved from the
resource-based view of the firm. Resource-based theorists view the firm as a unique
bundle of assets and resources that if employed in distinctive ways can create competitive advantage (Barney, 1991; Peteraf, 1993). The distinctive ways in which
firms manage these assets and resources can result in superior performance and
act as a durable source of competitive advantage. Core competence is important to
the study of outsourcing, as it has proposed the internal organisation of the firm as
the potential for competitive advantage. Obtaining, creating and developing certain
capabilities is central to the core competence approach and has important implications for what processes should be kept within the firm and which should be external to the firm. The ideas of core competence and its relationship with outsourcing
have been influenced by the work of Hamel and Prahalad (1994). They contend that
core competencies are not physical assets. Physical assets, no matter how innovative they may seem in the present, can be very easily replicated or become obsolete.
Instead, Prahalad and Hamel argue that the real sources of competitive advantage

are to be found in management's ability to consolidate corporate-wide technologies and production skills into competencies that empower individual businesses to adapt rapidly to changing business opportunities. They argue that core competencies are 'the collective learning in the organisation, especially how to co-ordinate diverse production skills and integrate multiple streams of technologies'.

However, operationalising the core competence concept in an outsourcing context has proved difficult as the concept involves, 'skills/ knowledge sets', 'root systems', 'unique sources of leverage', 'elements important in the long term', which appear vague and intangible. Owing to these difficulties, many companies have unknowingly relinquished their core competencies by cutting internal investment in what they mistakenly thought were 'cost centres' in favour of external service providers. In other words, the need to focus on core competencies has been operationalised for cost reduction reasons through the reduction of headcount. Determining which processes can be best performed by external service providers requires a good understanding of where the competitive advantage of an organisation resides (Barthelemy, 2003). However, rather than using outsourcing to build competitive advantage, companies are employing outsourcing to offload problem processes (McIvor, 2005). Organisations often decide that it is not necessary to allocate resources to tackle processes with which they are experiencing problems. In certain circumstances, where poor performance is a result of a lack of scale economies or knowledge of the process, outsourcing the process may be appropriate. For example, where a supplier can realise significant scale economies in a process through servicing the requirements of a number of customers, it is very difficult for the sourcing organisation to replicate such a position. However, in circumstances where poor performance is a result of poor management that can be addressed through an internal improvement initiative, then outsourcing can be fraught with risks. For example, these processes may be of significant value to the company currently and in the future, potentially contributing to the organisation's competitive advantage.

There are a number of additional reasons why strict adherence to the core competence approach to outsourcing can be problematic. The nature of some industries can make the emphasis on the distinction between core and non-core processes as the key motive for outsourcing inappropriate. For example, in rapidly changing industries technological innovations can render an advantage in a process obsolete almost overnight (Marshall et al., 2007). In these circumstances, outsourcing is driven more by the nature of the outsourcing contract and the management of the relationship between the sourcing organisation and the supplier. Furthermore, as most processes have elements that belong to the core business and elements that do not, adopting the core/non-core dichotomy can be difficult. Even when a process is considered to be 'non-core' to the organisation achieving competitive advantage, there are often implicit and tacit inter-dependencies with processes that are considered to be 'core' (Bryce and Useem, 1998; Mani et al., 2006). For example, when outsourcing a process an organisation may fail to account for both the formal and informal co-ordinating mechanisms that have allowed the organisation to perform the process internally in the past. The outsourcing of such a process can also have a detrimental effect upon the performance of core processes that remain within the organisation. Indeed, the failure to account for the tacit interdependencies between organisational processes is a potential risk of outsourcing in general.

2.8.3 LACK OF EMPHASIS ON PERFORMANCE MEASUREMENT IN OUTSOURCING

Whilst there is a growing body of literature focusing on outsourcing, the number of papers concerned with outsourcing and performance is still relatively small. In fact, limited research exists to guide practitioners on how to measure outsourcing performance. This is evident in many of the frameworks proposed in the literature. Early frameworks in this area tended to focus on outsourcing in a manufacturing context – the classic make-or-buy decision (Higgins, 1955; Culliton, 1956). These approaches were principally concerned with applying quantitative models to evaluate the decision. Many of the quantitative models have placed considerable emphasis on evaluating the costs associated with the decision which involves attempting to measure all the important costs associated with the two alternatives: make or buy (Gambino, 1990; Bassett, 1991; Ellis, 1992).

Transaction cost economics (TCE) has also influenced many of the approaches proposed in the literature in evaluating outsourcing decision (Aubert et al., 1996; Ngwenyama and Bryson, 1999; Vining and Globerman, 1999). TCE specifies the conditions under which an organisation should perform process internally within its boundaries and the conditions suitable for outsourcing the process (Williamson, 1975, 1985). At its most simplest, TCE argues that organisations should consider the level of transaction-specific investment in the economic exchange as the principal determinant of whether a process should be performed internally within the boundary of the organisation. Organisations will make the outsourcing decision on the basis of reducing transaction costs. As one would expect, proponents of outsourcing frameworks influenced by the transaction cost perspective argue that the optimal sourcing option will be chosen on the basis of transaction cost minimisation. Vining and Globerman's (1999) framework focuses on how an organisation assesses *ex ante* the potential governance costs that arise in outsourcing and how and in what circumstances governance costs can be reduced. However, some have challenged the predominance of cost considerations in the outsourcing decision with scant attention being given to how the decision impacts upon the long-term capabilities of the organisation (Holcomb and Hitt, 2007; McIvor, 2008).

A major source of difficulty for organisations when measuring outsourcing performance is that they have never effectively measured the performance of the process when it was performed internally. This is often the case when organisations have outsourced processes which they have been experiencing problems. For example, Shi (2007) has found that organisations have not developed effective metrics to measure the process performance. Furthermore, they have developed metrics for the first time when they outsource the process. A major risk of poor performance measurement in the outsourcing process is that organisations have no way of knowing whether the external service provider has performed the process better or worse than the internal department previously. Some have argued that organisations should create metrics to measure the quality of processes for a while and improve performance internally before outsourcing (Aron and Singh, 2005). Performance measurement is also an essential element of effective contracting. Barthelemy (2003) has found that many organisations have entered into outsourcing contracts without establishing objective performance measurement clauses. The lack of objective performance measures often leads to costly mistakes and long time periods before service providers can perform processes effectively. Performance requirements must be clearly established at the outset and incorporated into the contract. This will assist in ensuring that incentives can be built into the contract to encourage performance improvements and also improve the nature of the client–service provider relationship.

2.9   Requirements for an outsourcing framework

The previous section has identified the limitations of the existing outsourcing literature and practice. This section outlines the requirements for an outsourcing framework in order to address these limitations.

2.9.1   PERFORMANCE MEASUREMENT

Quelin and Duhamel (2003) have argued that a clear appreciation of the objectives and risks of outsourcing is an essential pre-condition to the formation of suitable outsourcing performance measurements. Whether an organisation decides to improve performance in a process via an internal improvement initiative or outsourcing, performance measurement is an important ingredient for success. A common classification of performance metrics is financial and non-financial, which tend to be firm specific. However, in an outsourcing context it is important to analyse performance at the level of the business process. In fact, there is increasing academic research that uses the process as the unit of analysis when investigating factors that contribute to performance, particularly in the service industries (Frei and Harker, 1999). For example, Silver (2004) argued that the traditional functional perspective should be expanded to a cross-functional process management perspective in line with the process orientation of major recent developments in the field, for example just in time (JIT), continuous improvement (TQM), business process reengineering (BPR), enterprise resource planning (ERP) and supply chain management (SCM). Silver (2004) argued that many important processes extend across functional boundaries. For example, it was reported that there have been many recent academic articles emphasising the importance of implementing SCM as part of a process orientation of management (Croxton et al., 2001). Performance measurement at the business process level makes sense because improvements in business processes will have a direct impact on operational performance. Because outsourcing has the objective of improving business processes, measurement of outsourcing performance should also focus at the business process level.

2.9.2 THE RESOURCE-BASED VIEW

The resource-based view is an important theory in enhancing our understanding of the outsourcing decision. In particular, the resource-based view can assist in the analysis of organisational capabilities, which can link outsourcing to organisational performance and in turn competitive advantage. It is possible to relate the resource-based view to analysing the capabilities of an organisation relative to competitors and suppliers in an outsourcing context. According to Barney (1999), a resource with the potential to create competitive advantage must meet a number of criteria including *value, rarity, imitability* and *organisation*. Resources and capabilities are considered valuable if they allow an organisation to both exploit opportunities and counter threats. Therefore, these resources should enable the organisation to meet the factors critical to success in their business environment. The rarity criterion is related to the number of competitors that possess a valuable resource. Clearly, where a number of competitors possess a valuable resource then it is unlikely to be a source of competitive advantage and therefore is a suitable candidate for outsourcing. A valuable resource that is unique amongst both current and potential competitors is likely to be a source of competitive advantage. Valuable and rare resources can be a source of competitive advantage and should be performed internally and developed. The imitability criterion is concerned with considering the ease with which competitors can copy a valuable and rare resource possessed by an organisation. In effect, this analysis is concerned with determining the sustainability of the competitive advantage in the resource. Finally, Barney (1999) argues that a firm must be *organised* to exploit its resources and capabilities. The organisation criterion includes a number of elements including the reporting structure, management control systems and compensation policies. It is important to emphasise that even though a firm may possess a range of valuable, rare and costly to imitate resources, ineffective organisation will prevent the full exploitation of these resources.

Many proponents of the resource-based view have argued that competitive advantage is created from resources and capabilities that are owned and controlled within a single organisation. Therefore, resources that are internal to the organisation drive competitive advantage. However, some scholars have extended the scope of the resource-based view to focus on resources that span the boundaries of the organisation (Das and Teng, 2000; Matthews, 2003) – sometimes referred to as the 'extended resource-based view'. Proponents of this literature propose it as a means of understanding how firms can gain and sustain competitive advantage. For example, Dyer and Singh (1998) argue that it is possible for organisations to combine resources in unique ways across organisational boundaries to obtain an advantage over their competitors. Firms can develop valuable resources by carefully managing relationships with external entities including suppliers, customers, government agencies and universities. Therefore, a firm can gain and sustain competitive advantage by accessing its key resources in a way that span the boundaries of the firm. Research has suggested that there is the potential for productivity improvements in the value chain when organisations are willing to make relation-specific investments and combine resources in unique ways (Dyer, 1996). Organisations that make relation-specific investments are able to combine resources in unique ways to generate relational rents and gain competitive advantage over organisations that are unable to do this.

2.9.3   THE STRATEGIC CONTEXT

Outsourcing has strategic implications for the organisation and as a consequence should be at the heart of business strategy. Outsourcing can be employed to achieve performance improvements along a number of dimensions including cost, quality, service and time-to-market. However, failure to place outsourcing within a strategic context will lead to a piecemeal approach based solely on attempts to reduce costs. Many organisations fail to establish clear strategic objectives on what they are intending to achieve and have no basis for evaluating the success of outsourcing. Rather than being approached strategically, it is often approached from a defensive position and in response to the actions of competitors. A key element of business strategy involves determining how an organisation should develop and accumulate the skills and capabilities that create and sustain competitive advantage both currently and in the future. However, a clear risk of outsourcing is that an organisation may outsource some of the skills and capabilities that are critical to future success – sometimes referred to as 'hollowing-out'. In fact, such a trend is extremely dangerous, as it not only threatens the future capability of an organisation but over time can also result in the decline in competitiveness of an industry. Therefore, considerable attention and effort should be given to ensuring that the future capability of the organisation is being considered when distinguishing between activities that should be kept in-house and those that should be outsourced. Placing outsourcing in a strategic context will ensure that it is linked to the overall mission and strategic objectives of the organisation.

2.10 Business services perspective

As already outlined many outsourcing frameworks have focused primarily on manufacturing. In a manufacturing context the focus has often been on component production and assembly. This is a relatively straightforward concept, as component production and assembly can be clearly demarcated and standardised. The outsourcing of these functions is facilitated by modular design and open product architecture. Suppliers are likely to exploit economies of scale across a broad customer base as opportunities arise, possibly even developing new capabilities to expand upstream or downstream in the supply chain. However, business services outsourcing is a different type of outsourcing concept, as business processes can very rarely be broken down as clearly as component production or assembly in a manufacturing context. Business services are services that are provided to other businesses, rather than directly to the public (Abramovsky et al., 2004). Examples of business services include computer services, professional services (legal, accountancy, market research, technical, engineering, advertising, human resources and consultancy), R&D, recruitment agencies and call centres. Between 1984 and 2001 the growth in the business services sector accounted for around one-third of the total output growth in the UK economy. Furthermore, there has been extensive outsourcing – both locally and offshore – in the area of business services. Rapid advances in ICTs have been a key driver towards outsourcing in this area. Despite the phenomenal growth of business services outsourcing, outsourcing as a strategic tool within the service industries has been given very little attention by researchers.

Background to the Development of the Outsourcing Framework

The first phase in the development of the outsourcing framework involved a thorough review of the literature. The next phase involved talking directly with practitioners to elicit their views on the key steps involved in the outsourcing process. A series of structured interviews with senior managers in a number of organisations was conducted. Interviews were carried out with senior managers from a range of business functions in each organisation in order to obtain a cross-functional perspective on the outsourcing process. As a result of these interviews and a review of the literature, an outsourcing framework was developed. The framework places particular emphasis on performance measurement in the outsourcing process. The framework encompasses a number of variables and seeks to capture the complexities of the outsourcing process. An overview of the outsourcing framework is illustrated in Figure 3.1. The issues associated with each stage in the framework will be fully discussed in Chapter 6. Figure 3.1 links the stages in the framework with the relevant sections of Chapter 5.

The principal proposition of this framework is that implementing a successful outsourcing strategy for a process must involve an analysis of a number of dimensions including relative capability in the process and contribution of the process to

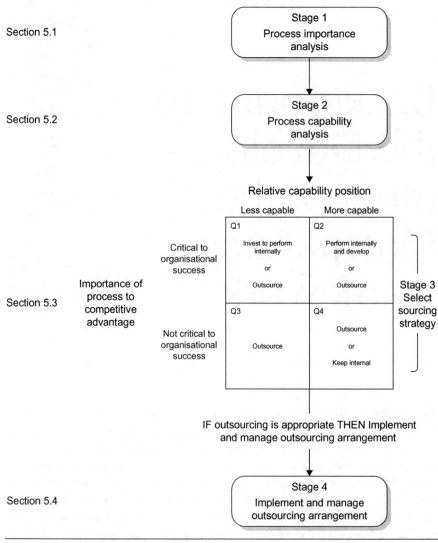

Figure 3.1   The outsourcing framework.

competitive advantage. Analysing each of these dimensions will provide an organisation with a number of sourcing strategies. The importance of considering these dimensions in outsourcing decisions is now discussed.

3.1 Relative capability position in the process

A key issue in competitive strategy involves understanding why one firm differs in performance from another. Some firms gain advantage over others because they can conduct certain organisational processes in a superior manner relative to their competitors. Furthermore, the superior performance in the process is considered sustainable where it is extremely difficult for competitors to replicate within a realistic timeframe or cost. In evaluating the suitability of processes for outsourcing, determining how well the organisation performs certain processes relative to competitors, and indeed suppliers, is a key issue. Therefore, this analysis is concerned with identifying the performance disparity between the sourcing organisation and potential external providers of the processes under scrutiny. It allows an organisation to focus on whether it will be detrimental to its competitive position to outsource certain organisational processes. It is also important to determine whether the organisation can achieve a sustainable competitive advantage by performing a critical process internally on an on-going basis. Clearly, if the organisation can perform such a process uniquely well, then this process should continue to be carried out internally. Part of this analysis involves understanding the sustainability of a superior performance position. In the case of critical processes, such an understanding will have a fundamental influence on the sourcing option chosen due to the implications for the competitive position of the organisation. Understanding the source of the advantage will provide a sound indication of the difficulties with attempting to replicate or surpass superior performance levels in the process.

3.2 Importance of the process to competitive advantage

This stage is concerned with assessing the importance of the process to competitive advantage. Determining the importance of a process to competitive advantage is central to the outsourcing process. Processes that are critical to competitive advantage and in which the organisations possesses a distinctive capability should remain internally and receive a considerable level of strategic attention in order to maintain such a position. Processes that are critical to competitive advantage have a major impact upon the ability of an organisation to achieve competitive advantage either through the ability to achieve a lower cost position and/or create higher levels of differentiation than competitors. Therefore, superior performance in such a process allows an organisation to offer sustained price reductions and/or differentiate the product or service in the eyes of the customer. Processes that are not critical to competitive advantage have a limited impact upon the ability of an organisation to achieve competitive advantage. Although these processes have to be performed well, any performance improvements achieved in such processes are unlikely to be a source of competitive advantage as they are not key differentiators in the eyes of customers when purchasing the product or service.

Practical Application of the Outsourcing Framework

The outsourcing framework was then applied in a UK financial services organisation over a 4 year period. This organisation offers a range of financial services including deposit taking, current account facilities, residual and commercial mortgages, and other tailored products and services. These services are offered across a number of segments including individuals, small- and medium-sized commercial and large corporate clients. This organisation was chosen for a number of reasons. The organisation had already outsourced a range of areas of their operations. Changes in both the internal and external environments of the organisation had led to the organisation outsourcing a range of processes in order to meet the increasing demands of its stakeholders. Furthermore, the research team had already established strong relationships with this organisation, which facilitated full access and participation in the research.

An action research approach was applied to this research. Action research involves combining utility for managers, measured by actions arising from the intervention, with the opportunity to research the problem area in depth (Mills et al., 2003). The action researcher is more than an independent observer and becomes an active participant in the subject of the research. Action research seeks to generate knowledge, recommend change and observe it put into practice to improve business practices and performance outcomes (Stringer, 1996). Action research operates in 'real time' and seeks to identify the complexities of the situation that it desires to change. Therefore, it is suited to a case study research approach where its methods are mainly inductive in nature. In this case, data gathered through case study analysis will focus on a range of sources of evidence including documentation, archival records, interviews, direct observation, participant observation and workshops. The evidence generated by these data collection methods was both quantitative and qualitative. Adopting this approach provided a detailed understanding of the factors involved in understanding the implications of performance measurement in the outsourcing decision. The action research approach adopted with the financial services organisation progressed through the following stages:

- The first stage of the research involved carrying out a number of workshops with senior management in the financial services organisation. During the workshop senior management were given an overview of the outsourcing process and the issues that should be considered in the decision-making process. An overview of the CSF method was provided along with how it assisted in identifying the relative importance of organisational processes. Senior management then developed CSFs and the relevant performance measures for their organisations in consultation with the research team. Using this approach, the relative importance of organisational processes was assessed.

- The next stage involved assessing the capability of the organisation in the processes chosen relative to external service providers. This involved considerable analysis including performance benchmarking as well as seeking the opinions of managers in the areas being examined. Based on this analysis, a number of sourcing strategies were implemented for each process examined. This involved carrying out workshops with senior management and management from the areas involved in order to understand the key issues and justify the choice of the most appropriate sourcing strategy. Throughout this process they worked together with the research team in applying the principles associated with the outsourcing framework.

- The final stage involved assessing the applicability of the framework and identifying lessons that could be learned from the exercise. This involved eliciting the opinions of staff at a number of levels in the financial services organisation.

Throughout the research project data were collected from a number of sources. First, the organisation provided access to a range of documented material. Archival data in the form of internal memoranda, annual reports, strategy documents, supplier evaluations, trade and internal company magazine articles were also collated. Second, data were collected via carrying out a series of in-depth face-to-face interviews with staff at a number of levels within the organisation. Interviews were carried out with both senior managers who were involved in formulating outsourcing strategies and with personnel from a range of functions at lower levels in each organisation who were involved in implementation. Semi-structured interviews took place with each of the personnel involved, with the intention that personnel would freely express their views and experiences on the process. The interviews normally lasted from 1 to 3 hours. Gathering this data involved a great deal of interaction between the researchers and the staff in the organisation.

In relation to data analysis, case studies were developed from both interviews undertaken with personnel involved in the outsourcing decisions and the archival data gathered. Using Eisenhardt's (1989) guidelines on case study analysis, within case analysis and cross-case analysis were carried out. These analyses were important in assessing the applicability of key elements of the outsourcing framework. As part of these analyses, follow-up interviews were undertaken to discuss both earlier responses and those of other informants. These interviews often involved additional questions based on information obtained from earlier interviews. A key strength of this approach was that it allowed the triangulation of data from multiple informants. Various charts, tables and figures were developed and used in the data analysis phase. Multiple sources of evidence including the interviews and archival data were used to triangulate data. Each case was further investigated through multiple interviews and additional visits to the case companies, to review the findings.

Chapter 5

The Outsourcing Framework in Action at the Financial Services Organisation

This section provides a detailed overview of the stages involved in the outsourcing framework. Case illustrations from the financial services organisation (FSO) are introduced at various stages in order to illustrate this framework in practice. Adopting this approach illustrates the practical implications of applying the framework. Based on this analysis, a number of important lessons for organisations integrating performance measurement consideration into the outsourcing process are identified.

5.1 Stage 1: Process importance analysis

This stage in the outsourcing process involves determining the level of importance of the processes that have to be performed to satisfy customer needs. Identifying critical processes involves understanding the major determinants of competitive advantage in the markets in which the organisation competes or might wish to compete. An analysis of the competitive environment and customer needs can have an important role in identifying which processes are critical for success. Critical processes will enable an organisation to differentiate itself from its competitors in the way in which it serves its customers. An understanding of critical processes is central to outsourcing evaluation. For example, where an organisation possesses a superior capability in a critical process relative to competitors or suppliers, it should continue to perform that process internally. Furthermore, the organisation must have a clear understanding of how sustainable this position is over time. Alternatively, where possible, processes that are not key influences on the ability of the organisation to achieve competitive advantage should be outsourced. Critical processes are those that can be used to build sources of advantage that are difficult and costly for competitors to replicate.

Segmenting the organisation into critical and non-critical processes

Assessing the contribution of a process to competitive advantage will involve distinguishing between processes that are critical and non-critical. For outsourcing purposes, critical and non-critical processes are defined as follows:

- *Critical processes*: These have a major impact upon the ability of an organisation to achieve competitive advantage either through the ability to reduce cost and/or create differentiation. Therefore, superior performance in such a process relative to competitors offers customers a unique value proposition. Consequently, the process is a source of competitive advantage. For example, an engine manufacturer may compete in markets where customers are increasingly demanding high standards of fuel economy, emissions and engine performance. Therefore, fuel systems and pistons are regarded as critical components – processes that are critical to fuel economy, emissions and performance.

- *Non-critical processes*: These have a limited impact upon the ability of an organisation to achieve competitive advantage. Although these processes are central to successfully serving the needs of customers in each market, any performance advantage obtained in such processes will not lead to a sustainable competitive advantage as competitors or suppliers can easily replicate this performance advantage.

Distinguishing between critical and non-critical processes in the context of outsourcing is important for the following reasons:

- Assessing the importance level of processes allows the organisation to determine whether outsourcing a process will maintain the competitive position of the organisation or act as a source of competitive advantage. For example, outsourcing a process such as catering or security that has limited or no impact upon why customers buy the products or services of the organisation is unlikely to have any impact upon competitive differentiation. Alternatively, employing outsourcing to achieve superior performance in a critical process has the potential to create competitive advantage. For example, an organisation may outsource a process whilst employing astute relationship mechanisms – either competitive or collaborative – that allow it to leverage potential benefits from a supplier that are unavailable to its competitors.

■ The importance level of a process is a valuable indicator of the level of resource and attention that should be given to managing that process. Employing definitions of critical and non-critical processes in this context provides a valuable basis for determining the level of attention that should be given to managing the outsourcing process. For example, a higher level of attention should be given to an outsourcing strategy that is designed to strengthen a critical process than the one of a non-critical process.

■ The importance level of processes is linked to the factors in the external business environment that can create business success. Also, these factors can change over time due to changes in customer preferences or improved competitive offerings. For example, an organisation may decide to perform a process internally because it is currently important in the eyes of the customer, that is one of the principal reasons why the customer purchases the product. However, over time that factor may diminish in importance in the eyes of the customer as competitors or suppliers become more proficient at performing the process, that is it is no longer a source of differentiation. In this case, it will be more prudent to outsource the process.

A useful technique for distinguishing between critical and non-critical processes in the context of outsourcing is the CSF methodology (McIvor, 2005). The CSF method is useful in an outsourcing context in that it can establish a direct link between outsourcing and the factors that influence business success. For example, CSFs are a very effective tool for providing information about customer needs and potential sources of competitive differentiation. The identification of CSFs can enable an organisation to determine the key processes that create value. The development of certain processes – either internally or externally with service providers – can enable an organisation to exploit market opportunities and in some cases create new opportunities in the competitive environment. By employing this technique in the outsourcing process, it is possible to obtain valuable insights into the types of capabilities that are likely to secure competitive advantage for an organisation.

5.1.1 THE CSF METHOD

Van Veen-Dirks and Wijn (2002) have found that the CSF methodology can help practitioners deal effectively with the tension between strategy implementation and formulation. The CSFs methodology is valuable in outsourcing evaluation and management in that it can establish a direct link between the potential sourcing options and the market. For example, market-oriented CSFs are a very effective tool for providing information about customer needs and potential sources of competitive differentiation. The CSF method provides a language that generates acceptance at the senior managerial level. It also can serve as a means of identifying important areas for strategic attention. By using performance measures to monitor the status of CSFs, changes in the market can be detected directly allowing appropriate management action to be taken. There are two key elements of the CSF methodology as given below.

Identification of CSFs

CSFs can be developed from both the mission statement of the organisation and from an evaluation of the organisation's competitive position. Hardaker and Ward (1987) have argued that a sound basis for the identification of CSFs is to consider the mission statement of the organisation. The mission statement of an organisation is a general statement of the purposes of an organisation and should express the overriding *raison d'etre* of the business. Using the mission statement as a basis, CSFs can be defined on the basis of what the organisation has to accomplish in order to achieve its mission. The competitive environment also has a significant impact upon the determination of CSFs. The level of competitive rivalry along with the threat of new entrants is likely to have an impact upon the CSFs chosen. For example, in industries where there is a high level of competitive rivalry, success can be heavily dependent upon pursuing aggressive cost reduction strategies.

Determine performance measures to monitor CSFs

Performance measures should be determined to allow the organisation to monitor progress on whether the CSFs are being met. For example, a retailer may identify a CSF as the development of excellent supplier relationships. In order to monitor progress on this CSF, performance measures may include sales per customer, number of complaints, number of inquiries, percentage on-time delivery and number of late payments. CSFs can also assist in determining what information is required in order to monitor the overall performance of the organisation.

5.1.2 ILLUSTRATION: CSFs IN ACTION AT THE FINANCIAL SERVICES ORGANISATION

Senior management in the FSO carried out a detailed analysis of the competitive environment and customer needs to identify CSFs. This analysis identified a number of major drivers of its competitive strategy, which are now outlined. The business strategy of the FSO has been influenced by a number of environmental changes. The financial services industry has seen a radical liberalisation of markets alongside a rapid development of technology, which provided new channels of distribution such as Internet banking, mobile lending, etc. These changes significantly increased the competition in financial markets and forced organisations to enhance the quality of customer choice and service. Competition from mutual fund companies, building societies and brokerage houses over the last 20 years has greatly affected the profitability of traditional consumer banking markets. The traditional boundaries in the industry have been gradually eroded, particularly within the banking sector where building societies have diversified into money transmission activities and the clearing banks have expanded into residential mortgage lending. Competition has been compounded by the removal of regulatory barriers to cross-border competition. This placed pressures on FSOs to reduce their operating costs. This requirement highlighted the necessity of developing a continuous performance improvement ethos within financial services institutions.

The intensity of competition in the industry has meant that it has been virtually impossible for any single FSO to dictate market prices. Downward pressure on prices has forced organisations to increase the value associated with each customer. Customer value in the financial services industry has been based primarily on the number of different products held by each customer. As organisations diversified and expanded their products and markets, issues of risk management have become increasingly important for profitability and stability. Revenue for FSOs has become much more dependent on achieving aggressive sales growth. This has necessitated the use of customer information to generate ever more sophisticated marketing strategies. There has been a drive to create a more positive attitude towards sales and marketing within the institutions particularly with regard to banking services. This has created new organisation structures. It has become increasingly common for the duties of business development and transaction processing to be dedicated roles. Most FSOs have centralised many business processes to remove duplication of effort whilst at the same time pursuing efficiency gains in many back-office processes.

Developments in technology have put pressure on FSOs to make the most efficient use of the multitude of delivery channels that are available. There has been a notable change in customer behaviour patterns in response to technological developments. Overall, the availability of technology has presented significant capital investment decisions for the financial services businesses. However, there has been a steady growth in the number of outsourcing service providers to the financial services industry. Such service providers have been offering front- and back-office processes, which have allowed FSOs to reduce capital investments in technology.

In addition, regulation has intensified in response to public and government demands for enhanced governance, accountability and transparency including a host of European Commission directives stemming from the Financial Services Action Plan (1999). Both government and the public have called for increased consumer protection. The Review of Banking Services in the UK was published in March 2000 to investigate the exposure of banks to competition law and it was believed that banks were much less regulated relative to other industries. The Financial Services and Markets Act (FSM Act) came into force in the UK in November 2001. Following the FSM Act the Financial Services Authority (FSA) took on its full authorities as the single regulator for the industry. In parallel with the FSM Act, financial regulatory law in the UK was radically updated and transformed on an integrated basis i.e. from late 2001 onwards, the FSA would act as sole regulator, one Act of Parliament was introduced, and a single Handbook of Rules and Guidance was prepared with a single point of contact for each organisation in the industry. This initiative has four main objectives; to promote market confidence, to facilitate the public in increasing their knowledge of the financial industry, to improve consumer protection and to decrease financial corruption. From November 2004, residential mortgages also became regulated products covering lending, administration, arranging and advising. The legislation also regulated the sale or administration of general insurance and retail investments.

In response to these drivers in the business environment in which the FSO operated, senior management developed the following CSFs:

■ *Low cost transactions*: This refers to the capability to manage cash and paper transactions (debits and credits on behalf of their customers). The capability to process credit applications is also an important element of this capability. Some of the processes related to this CSF include counter management in branches, automatic teller machines, Internet banking, customer credit application interviews and security perfection.

■ *Improve customer added value*: A critical element of the organisation's strategy has been to decentralise many of the administrative processes in branches and focus more resource on direct customer sales services such as credit assessment and delivery, financial advice and share dealing. Some of the processes central to this CSF include customer relationship management, research of the marketplace and credit assessment.

■ *Availability of expert resources*: This is central to achieving its business strategy. Processes central to achieving this CSF include recruitment, training and development, personal development programmes and staff attitude surveys.

■ *Importance of the process to innovation*: The need for new and innovative products is increasing in the financial services sector. Also, the high level of regulation in the financial services sector means that new products have to be tested rigorously before release to the market. In the development of new products, the organisation either develops new products internally or forms strategic alliances in order to enhance its product and service offering. Important processes for this CSF include research of the marketplace and customer relationship management.

■ *Process contribution to customer understanding/analysis*: The trend towards a greater focus on building customer relationships has led to the need for a greater understanding of customer behaviour and needs. The organisation requires a greater knowledge of what products their customers currently use, products that their current customers are buying from competitors and the products that their customers are unaware that the organisation can provide. Some of the processes central to this CSF include analysis of customer satisfaction surveys, advertising and creating awareness, and understanding customer requirements.

■ *Impact on governance and regulation*: The FSA regulates the financial services sector in order to prevent malpractice in a number of areas including money laundering and offering of poor advice. Compliance with the FSA involves acting fairly in dealings with customers and assisting customers in understanding how their financial products and services work. Compliance with these regulations is perceived as enhancing the brand image of the FSO. Providing advice, confidentiality and excellent customer service are central to building this brand. Important processes for this CSF included compliance with FSA guidelines on 'best advice' and 'money laundering', keeping up to date on legislation and adherence to the banking codes.

Senior management in the FSO identified the factors that were believed to be critical to the success of the business strategy. Furthermore, senior management wanted to limit the CSFs to a maximum of six in order not to dilute their importance. The process of identification was very thorough. In fact, the FSO sought opinions beyond the senior management team through a process of in-depth interviews with branch staff. Whilst the action research methodology permitted the research team to influence the selection of CSFs, it was felt that the CSFs being classified by the FSO were in line with the key business issues being faced by retail banks in the UK at the time. For example, a practitioner-based study carried out by Nelson-Hall in 2005 entitled 'BPO Opportunities in the Banking Sector' interviewed 60 banking chief financial officers to ascertain their attitudes to business issues and the opportunities for outsourcing. Table 5.1 shows the six issues that were highlighted as being critical. These issues corresponded closely with those identified by the case study organisation. These issues have remained critical to the banking industry as

Table 5.1   Issues faced by retail banks

Critical business issue	Proportion (%)
Need to adapt to increasingly competitive environment	100
Need to develop high-appeal products	93
Need to improve customer service	67
Need to reduce cost base	40
Need for improved compliance with regulations	30
Need for geographic expansion	17

Source: Nelson Hall (2005).

reported in the 2007 Nelson-Hall report of BPO opportunities in this industry. In addition, the need to coordinate delivery across multiple channels and to improve business processes has been added as a critical issue. This focus on business processes provides further currency with regard to the emphasis on outsourcing at the process level.

5.1.3   Using the CSFs to Determine Process Importance

CSFs – as determined by an analysis of the competitive environment and customer needs – should translate into a number of critical processes that create value for the organisation. The first step in this analysis involves determining how specific processes contribute to the achievement of the CSFs. For example, a CSF such as 'the operation of a cost-effective and safe manufacturing operation' needs to be clearly defined in terms of what it exactly means. In effect, this involves identifying the underpinning capabilities that are critical to achieving organisational success through each of the CSFs. Many of the processes identified will have some impact upon the CSFs. However, it is necessary to distinguish between the importance level of each process. One approach proposed by Keith Ward (1990) is to map the processes and their impact upon each CSF. The process should begin with identifying the processes that impact upon each CSF. It is likely that one process will impact upon a number of CSFs. A reliable indicator of the importance is the number of CSFs the process impacts upon. Ward's (1990) methodology regards critical processes as those that are central to the future success of the company as indicated by the count scores on the importance for the CSFs. However, this approach should be applied with care and in particular should be combined with the knowledge and experience of key decision makers within the organisation. This process of identifying the importance level of processes should be carried out by senior management along with inputs from teams from lower levels in the organisation. Each team should encompass a broad section of members – functionally, divisionally and hierarchically. It is important that the participants in the process work closely in group sessions to ensure that strong debate takes place.

5.1.4   Illustration: Using CSFs to Determine Process Importance at the FSO

This illustration outlines how the FSO used the CSFs identified to assess process importance. This proved to be an extremely challenging aspect of the analysis. Ward's (1990) methodology was used as a guide in this process, which involved mapping the underpinning processes and assessing their impact upon each CSF as shown in Figure 5.1. The left side of the matrix indicates the processes that have to be performed to achieve organisational success, whilst the right side of the matrix is used to assess both the importance and performance level of the process. A reliable indicator used to assess the importance of a process involved summing the number of CSFs the process impacts upon as shown in column (A). An assessment of organisational performance in the process was made as shown in column (B) of the matrix varying from A (no need for improvement) to E (still has to be developed). It is not uncommon to weigh business issues and CSFs and practitioner-based researchers such as Nelson-Hall attempted to do so. However, in this case study, there were only six factors highlighted and it was felt that they were all critical making any weighing exercise largely academic.

Although the matrix in Figure 5.1 might suggest that the process was well structured, this was certainly not the case. This part of the analysis led to considerable debate and discussion on the relative importance of each process. A difficulty encountered was the interdependencies between certain processes such as mortgages and securities which made it extremely difficult to define explicitly the impact of a single process on each CSF. Furthermore, this stage of the analysis led to the organisation re-thinking definitions of current processes in order to create greater clarity. However, the analysis was found to be valuable as it allowed the organisation to prioritise and identify areas of the business that required action of which outsourcing was a potential option.

Two critical and two non-critical processes were explored further and the results are presented in Table 5.2.

The two critical processes are money transmission (over the counter financial transactions) and mortgage processing (mortgage application and review process). The two non-critical processes are foreign exchange (foreign currency transactions) and cheque clearing (a system which enables cheques to be passed between bank branches and between different banking organisations to exchange funds). These

Critical success factors	Low-cost transactions	Improve customer-added value	Availability of expert resources	Importance of process to innovation	Process contribution to customer analysis	Impact on governance and regulation	(A) Count	(B) Process quality
Processes								
Money transmission	X	X	X	X	X	X	6	D
Credit delivery – mortgage processing	X	X	X	X	X	X	6	E
Communication process		X	X	X	X	X	5	B
Research and understand the marketplace		X		X	X	X	4	B
Sales training		X	X	X	X	X	5	C
Customer satisfaction surveys		X		X			2	C
Updating customer profiles		X				X	2	C
Understanding customer requirements		X	X	X			3	C
Credit assessment skills		X	X	X	X	X	5	A
Advertising		X		X			2	B
Customer relationship management		X	X	X	X		4	C
Recruitment		X	X				2	B
Training and development		X	X	X	X	X	5	B
Remuneration/Retention		X		X			2	A
Undertaking staff attitude surveys				X			1	A
Legal compliance process						X	1	B
Foreign exchange transactions	X	X				X	3	E
Cheque clearing	X		X			X	3	B

Figure 5.1   CSFs and the process importance matrix for the FSO.

processes were primarily chosen as a result of the low score obtained for process quality, indicating a significant opportunity for process improvement. However, cheque clearing was chosen due to its requirement for significant capital expenditure. In addition, it was felt that there were a number of existing service providers that had the potential to offer these specific critical and non-critical processes and that the outsourcing analysis would provide an opportunity to benchmark the bank's current business practices in these four processes.

Table 5.2 Process assessment at the FSO

	Critical – mortgage processing	Critical – money transmission via branch counters	Non-critical – foreign exchange	Non-critical – cheque clearing
Process Summary	■ Mortgage processing is a significant proportion of FSO's portfolio. ■ Continued growth in mortgage business is placing strain on processing ability at branches and head office. ■ Current difficulties include: high dependence on Mortgage Services Unit; disjointed work flows; reactive and crisis workload management in the mortgage centre; incomplete application with a high rework rate (60%). ■ Therefore, considered 'critical'.	■ Considered a loss leader due to high volume of low-value transactions and significant operating costs. ■ Currently each branch has a minimum of two teller positions. ■ 70% of existing customer base do not pay fees. ■ Therefore, considered 'critical'.	■ Declining demand for foreign exchange services due to technology changes and increasing competition from foreign exchange specialists. ■ The offering of this service was not considered to be a source of competitive differentiation in the marketplace. ■ There were a number of specialist service providers available. ■ Therefore, considered 'non-critical'.	■ Not perceived as an area of the business that could generate revenue for the company. ■ An area of the business where considerable improvements to quality and service could be realised with the introduction of new technology. ■ Initially, the company believed that more efficient external service providers in the supply market existed. ■ Therefore, considered 'non-critical'.

■ 5.2 Stage 2: Assessing process capability

A major part of outsourcing evaluation involves determining whether an organisation can achieve superior performance levels internally in critical processes on an ongoing basis. Clearly, if the organisation can perform the process uniquely well, then this process should continue to be carried out internally. However, many organisations assume that because they have always performed the process internally, it should remain that way. In many cases, closer analysis may reveal a significant disparity between their internal capabilities and those of the world's best suppliers and competitors. Organisations considering outsourcing must rigorously evaluate their capabilities internally and in relation to both their suppliers and competitors. Analysis from a process perspective is important given that organisations are increasingly positioning themselves in specific parts of the industry chain to gain competitive advantage. This analysis is concerned with identifying disparity between the sourcing organisation and potential external sources.

This type of analysis can identify sources of competitive advantage that can be exploited more fully by further developing certain processes. It also assists in revealing weaknesses that need to be addressed – either through internal improvement or outsourcing – in order to become more competitive. It can allow an organisation to focus on whether it will be detrimental to their competitive position to outsource processes such as research and development, design, engineering, manufacturing or assembly, both in the short and long term. Determining the capability of the sourcing organisation in relation to competitors or suppliers involves an analysis of the following:

- ■ *Cost analysis*: Part of this analysis involves comparing the costs of sourcing the process internally and from an external supplier. Also, an assessment of the relative cost position of the sourcing organisation in relation to both suppliers and competitors in the processes under scrutiny should be undertaken. An assessment of costs can form a significant part of capability analysis.

- ■ *Benchmarking*: This can assist in determining performance levels in the processes under scrutiny. Organisations considering outsourcing must rigorously evaluate their capabilities in relation to suppliers and competitors. This analysis involves a structured benchmarking approach to assessing the organisation's capabilities relative to potential suppliers and competitors. Benchmarking also involves consideration of the cost position relative to competitors and suppliers.

The level of analysis undertaken in relation to capability analysis will depend upon the level of importance of the process. Processes regarded as critical will require extensive analysis of performance levels in relation to both competitors and suppliers. As well as the importance of the process under scrutiny, the manner in which capability analysis is undertaken will also be influenced by the priorities of the sourcing organisation. These priorities may have been determined on the basis of the following:

■ The organisation may have identified a number of critical processes where it feels its performance is lacking in comparison to external sources. Therefore, urgent action is required in order to determine the significance of this disparity in performance.

■ The organisation may have identified a number of lesser important processes that it considers as potential candidates for outsourcing.

■ Organisational difficulties in certain areas may require rapid performance improvements. For example, complaints about some aspect of customer service may have precipitated the need for action whether through improving the process internally or outsourcing it to a supplier.

5.2.1   ILLUSTRATION: PROCESS COST ANALYSIS IN ACTION AT THE FSO

This illustration outlines how the FSO assessed the processing costs associated with mortgages. The ability to process mortgage applications quickly and accurately was a major priority for the FSO – due to a phenomenon sometimes referred to as 'churning'. Churning involves the loss of mortgage business to other providers during the life of the loan. This has become a major issue for many FSOs as competitive pressure from the pro-active re-brokering of mortgages by building societies and intermediaries has increased in recent years. Customers are often offered better terms by other lending institutions and are encouraged by the financial press to seek better mortgage deals. The problem for any organisation losing business of this nature is that it incurs considerable costs in the first few years; thus losing a mortgage in the early years means that profits are lost. Churning had become a major problem for the FSO that participated in this research. For example in 2003, 13.2% of its mortgage business was lost, and therefore in order to compensate for this loss new business had to be found. The FSO had calculated that if the level of churn reached 20%, it would need to sanction 5,888 new mortgages per annum in order to achieve sales targets. Therefore, it had to ensure that it had to limit the loss of customers as a result of taking too long to process their applications or being non-competitive with regard to price. A key part of addressing this problem involved understanding the costs involved in processing mortgages. An example of how the FSO assessed the cost of their mortgage application process is shown in Table 5.3.

From Table 5.3 it can be seen that on average it was costing the FSO £550 to process a mortgage application. The mortgages sold outside the branch network cost £20 more than those sold at a branch and this is due to relatively higher staff and marketing costs. Furthermore, insurance was not being sold outside of the

Table 5.3 Mortgage processing cost analysis

	Sold at branch	Sold outside branch network	Totals per annum	Sister organisation
Direct costs	£000	£000	£000	£000
Staff (total)	3,464	1,782	5,246	5,469
Marketing	231	118	349	
Procurement and legal fees	558	288	846	
Other	n/a	n/a	n/a	459
Total costs	4,253	2,188	6,441	5,928
Income (net)				(not available)
Mortgage	10,303	2,975	13,278	
Insurance	249	0	249	
Total income	10,552	2,975	13,527	
Surplus of income over expenditure	6,299	787	7,086	
Number of products sold	7,896	3,882	11,778	31,500
Average revenue per product sold	1.33	0.76	1.15	
Average cost per product sold	0.54	0.56	0.55	0.188
Average margin per product sold	0.79	0.20	0.60	
Number of staff	51	25	76	180
Mortgages processed per staff member per annum	155	155	155	175
Turnaround time	14 days	14 days	14 days	7 days

Notes:
The figures have been altered in the interests of confidentiality; furthermore, the sister organisation's figures have been converted from Euro to sterling.
Staff costs include the salaries of staff at branches and at head office, plus any overtime payments. Overtime is counted as a direct cost as it is a necessity.
Procurement and legal fees are deemed to be a central cost. For convenience they have been allocated on a proportional basis; that is products sold.
The breakdown of costs such as marketing and procurement and legal fees were not available for the sister organisation; however, it had another category, 'other', which might include these costs.

branch network, which means there is greater opportunity to increase the revenue in a branch. However, the value per product is far greater in the branches, averaging £1,304.84 compared to £766.36 sold outside and this is reflected in the much higher margin per product sold. Therefore, the branch network is far more effective at selling mortgages of a higher value. In terms of number of items sold, those being sold outside the network are broadly in line with the costs they incur. Products sold via other means generate 34% of the costs and account for 33% of sales volume.

The method used by the FSO to calculate cost per product sold involves adding together all the costs associated with processing a mortgage, splitting them into in-house and other, and dividing them by the number of products sold. Therefore the cost of any mortgage applications that were not converted into sales are being absorbed into the costs of those that are. Thus the bank was not looking at a process cost per product, but the total cost of an actual sale. Using the data above the bank also calculated the net income per product sold and also the margin (surplus of income over expenditure) per product sold and used them as a baseline for benchmarking purposes. When it compared the average cost (£550) of processing a mortgage application to one of its European sister organisations, it found that the average cost per product sold was far smaller at £188. Despite the fact that the sister operation benefited from economies of scale through processing a greater number of mortgages and was a lot more automated, there were clearly lessons to be learnt. The operating costs of the FSO were too high and this was having a detrimental impact on its profit margins.

Given the confidentiality issues surrounding the cost information provided, it was difficult to break down the direct costs into any other categories or match them against the three main activities, that is core (essential for the business to work effectively and efficiently), diversionary (the cost of failure) and support (those that enable the core activities to take place). Although classed as a direct cost by the FSO, marketing is usually categorised as a support activity. Likewise the FSO classed all staff costs as direct, yet it could be stated that overtime is a diversionary activity, as the fact it is being paid is because the allocated members of staff cannot cope with the workload within their normal hours of work. However, it can be assumed that the legal and procurement fees are due to core activities being undertaken. It is more straightforward to make a comparison between the staff costs of the FSO and its sister organisation, relative to the number of products sold, that is total staff costs divided by the number of products sold. The financial organisation staff cost per product sold was £445 (with those being sold at the branch costing £439 and those outside the network costing £459), whereas the sister operation is far more efficient as staff costs were £174 per product sold.

The lower half of Table 5.3 provides details of the productivity and efficiency of the two different sets of staff – as can be seen there is no difference between the mortgages processed per staff member per annum or the turnaround time within the FSO. However, there is a significant difference between the speed of process-ing mortgages, with the sister organisation being a lot faster (7 days as opposed to 14 days). What is noteworthy, however, is a fairly small difference in productiv-ity. Despite all the automation employed by the sister organisation each member of staff only processes 20 more mortgages per annum (a difference of 13%). Therefore it can be concluded that the members of staff at the FSO do not necessarily have to work harder, but just be more efficient in their working practices.

Limitations to cost analysis

There are a number of limitations to the cost analysis undertaken:

1. The FSO only provided direct costs. Therefore, overheads were not included although these would have impacted on the profit margins. Furthermore, the costs of accommodation were a lot higher in the sister organisation and thus the differences in cost per product were not as great as those displayed in Table 5.3.

2. The FSO did not use other well-known methods to analyse costs when pro-viding the financial figures (e.g. controllable/uncontrollable, avoidable/una-voidable) and thus it was difficult to get a full picture of costs. For example, marketing was classed as a direct cost, yet most organisations would class it as an indirect cost or overhead.

3. The information provided for both the FSO and the sister organisation and also for the FSO's internal and external operations (i.e. outside the branch network) was not always directly comparable, and thus a number of assumptions had to be made. The gaps in information were as follows:
   - The legal and procurement costs for the FSO were not broken down; therefore they were allocated between sold at branch/sold outside branch on a pro rata basis, which may not have been totally accurate.
   - No revenue costs were provided for the sister organisation, and thus it was not possible to calculate average revenue per product sold or average margin per product sold.
   - No marketing or legal and procurement costs were provided for the sis-ter organisation. They did have another category, which was simply called 'other', but there was no way of telling if this included marketing and legal and procurement costs.

5.2.2 PROCESS BENCHMARKING

An important element of capability analysis in the outsourcing process involves considering costs and the relative performance along a number of other dimensions such as quality, flexibility and service. Analysis along these additional dimensions is important given the experiences of organisations that have embarked upon outsourcing primarily on the basis of costs. For example, initial analysis may reveal that a supplier possesses a lower cost position whilst at the same time being weaker in areas such as quality and service. Organisations must have an understanding of the key measures that indicate performance in a process relative to suppliers or competitors.

5.2.3 INTEGRATING BENCHMARKING INTO THE OUTSOURCING PROCESS

It is important to understand and prioritise the processes under scrutiny in order to integrate benchmarking into the outsourcing process. It is not feasible to undertake an extensive benchmarking exercise for each process under scrutiny. In fact, the evaluation of outsourcing for an organisation is likely to focus on one or a limited number of processes as a starting point rather than an evaluation of every organisational process. The prior experience of the organisation in the area of benchmarking is a key consideration. When it is the organisation's first experience with benchmarking, it may be beneficial to undertake a brief and highly focused exercise that promises to deliver a high impact. Also, the type of process will have a significant influence on the way in which outsourcing evaluation can proceed in terms of capability analysis as outlined in the following examples:

- *Non-critical*: The sourcing organisation may approach a supplier with which it is currently doing business in order to determine if the supplier is interested in taking on an increased level of business in a particular product area. The supplier may already have the necessary capability in this area. This increased business may be in the form of a portfolio of components that the organisation wishes to completely outsource and close down the internal production source.
- *Critical*: In the case of a more critical process, the sourcing organisation may have to undertake a rigorous analysis of potential external sources to determine performance levels.

Each of these types of processes has different implications for the depth of analysis that should be undertaken. For example, in the case of a critical process, the capability analysis may involve the following comparisons:

- The sourcing organisation may compare its own performance in the process in terms of cost, quality and delivery against the supplier. This analysis may also extend to other suppliers in the supply market.
- As well as considering the performance of suppliers, the sourcing organisation may compare its own performance in the process against numerical performance indicators established and reported in public sources.

■ Along with external analysis, the organisation may undertake some historical comparisons in order to determine any significant changes in performance levels.

A number of the critical aspects involved in undertaking a comprehensive benchmarking exercise for outsourcing purposes are given below. It will concentrate on those aspects of benchmarking which have a particular impact on outsourcing evaluation.

I Benchmarking approach

This involves deciding who should undertake the benchmarking the exercise. The sourcing organisation can either use internal staff alone or involve external consultants to assist in undertaking the benchmarking exercise. A team should be formed to carry out the benchmarking of the processes under scrutiny. This team will be composed of both personnel involved in outsourcing evaluation such as senior management as well as representatives from the process under scrutiny.

II Process analysis

From an outsourcing perspective it is important to understand and analyse the process under scrutiny. The level of analysis will significantly depend upon the importance of the process. In the case of a process deemed to be of critical importance, it is necessary to conduct extensive analysis to determine the strategic options in terms of either internal improvement or using an external service provider. This more extensive analysis should involve carrying out the following tasks:

■ identification of the people and their roles in the process;

■ determining the role of suppliers in the process;

■ mapping and documenting the process by interviewing relevant people involved in the process and analysing organisation documents and reports.

Process maps are detailed diagrams comprising a flowchart of tasks and processes that make up some process. They also contain information for each step in the process including key input requirements, resource requirements, critical controls and constraints on the process, required outputs, performance levels or standards and customer requirements (Foot, 1998). Obtaining co-operation from the staff involved in the process can significantly enhance the validity of the process map. Process maps can also be used to compare performance across organisations to identify areas for improvement.

As a result of mapping the process a key outcome is the identification of performance metrics. This is necessary because before comparing performance with external sources, a clear understanding of internal performance is required. The choice

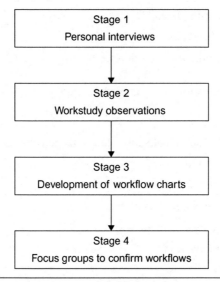

Figure 5.2   The stages involved in the analysis of the mortgages process.

of key metrics to be used for benchmarking purposes must be based upon how well they measure process performance, which in turn contributes to the overall success of the organisation. When searching for metrics it may be prudent to select metrics that are already in use in the organisation and that can be related to the CSFs or drivers of business success.

5.2.4   ILLUSTRATION: PROCESS ANALYSIS IN ACTION AT THE FSO

As part of the benchmarking exercise the FSO carried out a detailed analysis of the mortgages process and followed a four-stage process as illustrated in Figure 5.2. The analysis undertaken in each of these stages is now discussed.

Step 1: Personal interviews

Semi-structured interviews were conducted with each member of the mortgages services unit staff (MSU). The objective of each interview was to obtain information on the job role of each person and his/her experience. This would provide an overview of both the processes involved and the role of personnel. The following information was gathered in relation to the analysis of each process:

■   understanding of procedures and work systems;

■   understanding of information technology used to support the process;

■ explanation of reporting lines;

■ communication procedures;

■ description of any initiatives to improve the process.

The following information was gathered in relation to the analysis of each member of staff:

■ a description of the individual's job role and responsibilities;

■ duration of service in this role;

■ extent of training provided;

■ level of management support available;

■ assessment of time-management skills;

■ level of personal motivation;

■ career opportunities.

Each individual was asked to submit a sample of all documentation, which they used or had access to. In addition, if the individual made use of an information system, an overview of the system was conducted to assess ease of use and robustness against input errors.

Step 2: Work-study observations

Once the information from the personal interviews were gathered and analysed, work-study analysis was carried out to observe the mortgages process and associated sub-processes in action. These observations proved to be a very valuable mechanism for understanding the processes. In addition, they highlighted that there was inadequate flexibility in the system to cope with absenteeism either due to planned annual leave or unplanned illness. Such issues had not been raised during the personal interviews in the previous stage. Observations also revealed that staff training sessions did not actually take place with the frequency that interviews with personnel had suggested. Observing staff perform their jobs also revealed additional problems in terms of working conditions and a lack of basic equipment. It was also evident that some key staff spent the majority of their time answering branch queries over the telephone, which prevented them from performing their operational duties. The FSO realised that the requirements of the mortgages process had evolved over time and that new requirements and changes appeared to have been included on an incremental basis. There was a lack of emphasis on formally documenting the changing requirements of the branches and changes to the process. Work-study observation was the first step in assessing the performance of the process and provided the opportunity to identify bottlenecks, delays and duplication of effort.

Step 3: The development of workflow charts

Undertaking workflow analysis involved documenting each step in each process. This was facilitated by the observations in the previous stage where each staff member was observed through their day-to-day duties and each step in the current process recorded. The next stage involved employing various modelling techniques to identify the essential aspects of each process and sub-process. Workflow diagramming methods such as cross-functional workflows and cause and effect diagrams were created to visually represent the business processes. Flowcharts indicating the flow of materials, people and information through each sub-process were produced. With regard to mortgages processing, 10 A4 sub-process flowcharts were produced. These included charts for the sub-processes of mortgages application processing, sanctioning, completions, deeds-in, deeds-out, redemption quotations, capital reduction, full settlement and maintenance. A sample workflow chart for mortgages processing is illustrated in Appendix 1. The procedure involved determining the distinctive tasks required to accomplish the process objectives, choosing the ideal sequence that tasks should follow and determining who should be responsible for performing them. In addition to highlighting areas for process improvements, the flowcharts greatly assisted the development of performance measures for the process.

Step 4: Focus groups to confirm workflows

Once the process flowcharts had been developed, focus groups consisting of members of the Business Transformation Unit and key employees within the Mortgages Service Unit were formed. Forming these focus groups accomplished a number of objectives. First, the opinions of staff members were required to verify the workflows. Once this had been achieved, the processes were critically evaluated to identify problems or deficiencies and highlight any duplication of effort. Ideas for process improvements that would enhance quality and speed of throughput were identified and evaluated.

Step 5: Identification of performance metrics

An important outcome of the process evaluation is the development of performance measures. The project team spent a considerable amount of time with senior management and staff from each area of evaluation in order to ensure that the appropriate measures were identified. Table 5.4 provides an illustration of the performance metrics for money transmission, mortgages, foreign exchange and cheque clearing processes used by the FSO.

III Potential partner identification

Once processes have been mapped and understood, suitable benchmark partners should be found. Based on the mapped processes and the metrics developed, the development of a partner profile can assist in identifying companies carrying out

Table 5.4 Process performance measures in the FSO

	Critical: money transmission via branch counters	Critical: mortgage processing	Non-critical: foreign exchange	Non-critical: cheque clearing
Typical performance measures	■ Staff costs ■ Number of cash differences/period ■ Output per teller ■ Number of customers shifting to automated channels (e.g. phone and Internet banking) ■ Sales of other financial services (e.g. insurance and unsecured loans) ■ Customer satisfaction	■ Number of draw-downs ■ Percentage straight-to-offer ■ Percentage of redemptions ■ Application sanctioning speed ■ Speed of redemptions ■ Speed of overall turnaround ■ Customer satisfaction ■ Cost of processing	■ Volume of transactions ■ Staff costs ■ Number of cash differences ■ Customer waiting period	■ Accuracy of out-clearing and debit in-clearing ■ Accuracy of credit referencing ■ Accurate reconciliation of settlement ■ Turnaround speed of out-clearing and debit in-clearing ■ Speed of credit referencing ■ On-time completion of settlements

similar processes. Ideally, the organisation should benchmark against partners that are best-in-class in the process under scrutiny whether they are competitors, suppliers or organisations in other industries. However, the benchmarking partner chosen may be influenced more by the willingness of the partner to become involved than on their level of competence on the process under scrutiny. For example, this stage may be driven primarily by the ease of access that can be obtained from the potential benchmarking partner. In the context of outsourcing evaluation, the most competent service provider of the process is a valuable benchmarking partner. Information from service providers can be much more readily obtained than from competitors who are likely to have a natural reluctance to share commercially sensitive information.

In relation to competitors, benchmarking can act as an imperative for strategic action. For example, if the organisation establishes the performance benchmark for its competitors, then this can serve as a reliable indicator of competitive advantage. Also, benchmarking against competitors may reveal practices that are not worth attempting to replicate or surpass. Where the sourcing organisation finds that competitors are more competent, it has the following options:

■ In the case of a process deemed to have a high level of importance, then the organisation may attempt to develop the capability and improve to match or surpass competitor performance. Alternatively, the organisation may decide to select a supplier to perform the process.

■ In the case of a process deemed to have a low level of importance, then it may be more prudent for the organisation to consider outsourcing the process.

In relation to the use of best-in-class partners across other industries, access may be more readily achievable than that from direct competitors. With full access obtained it may then be possible to determine whether there is the potential to improve performance rather than considering the outsourcing option. Alternatively, the exercise may reveal too significant a disparity in performance that may force the sourcing organisation to consider outsourcing to a more competent service provider. Figure 5.3 illustrates the relationship between the resource involved in acquiring information and its value to outsourcing evaluation.

IV Data collection and analysis

Effective benchmarking involves ensuring that the right information is collected and then analysed. The first phase involves designing a questionnaire based on the partner profile. The benchmarking questionnaire should be a clear, formal agreement and understanding about what data and information are to be collected and shared. In relation to the level of access to and use of confidential information, rules need to be agreed by the partners. As well as a questionnaire, internal reports, site visits and interviews can be carried out with key staff within the partner organisation.

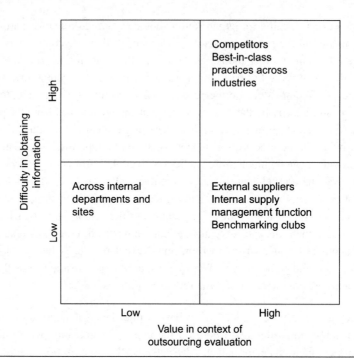

Figure 5.3 The difficulty of obtaining information and its impact upon outsourcing evaluation. *Source*: McIvor (2005).

It is important to note that the success of the benchmarking exercise depends upon the organisation understanding the results and consequences. In the context of outsourcing evaluation, the outcome of the exercise is likely to lead to significant change in the management of the organisation both internally and externally into the supply chain.

V Performance gap analysis

The benchmarking exercise should yield one of the following three scenarios:

- *Parity*: No significant difference in performance between the sourcing organisation and competitors or suppliers.
- *Internal more competent*: In this scenario internal performance is superior to that of either competitors or suppliers.
- *External more competent*: The performance of either competitors or suppliers is superior to that of the sourcing organisation.

Effective analysis will enable the organisation to determine how its performance compares with external sources. Essentially, the organisation has to identify the performance gap revealed by the performance analysis. It is important to identify and understand the underpinning performance indicators that explain the existence of the gap. Benchmarking can assist in identifying the potential strategic sourcing options that will lead to improvement in the performance of the process under scrutiny. It is possible to align benchmarking with the dimensions of performance that are critical to competitive advantage. It can be seen that there is a clear link between benchmarking and the overall business strategy of the organisation. As well as alerting management to potential outsourcing opportunities, it can also act as a vehicle to understanding whether processes can be improved internally.

5.2.5 ILLUSTRATION: THE EXPERIENCES OF THE FSO WITH BENCHMARKING IN THE OUTSOURCING PROCESS

This illustration integrates the various aspects of benchmarking discussed in the previous section and examines its application in the area of mortgages in the FSO. A key element of the competitive strategy of the FSO involved increasing its market share in the rapidly growing mortgage market. However, the mortgages unit was under-performing and was not in a position to allow the FSO to achieve this strategic objective. The costs associated with managing the unit were increasing and turnaround times for processing mortgages were also increasing. This was impacting upon the speed with which the organisation could develop and market new mortgage products. Senior managers realised that this area would have to be improved and thus outsourcing was considered a potential option in the initial stages of the analysis. Therefore, a number of senior managers were tasked with devising a plan to improve this area of the business. A key aspect of this analysis involved undertaking a benchmarking exercise to assess internal performance and generate potential sourcing options for improving performance.

Prior to benchmarking, the FSO undertook an analysis of its own internal mortgages unit. Although senior managers were aware of some of the problems through monthly reports, the analysis carried out revealed major problems, which would require significant attention. The case illustration in Section 5.2.4 has already provided some background on how they analysed the mortgage process and the problems they found. For example, they identified disjointed processes, a lack of an effective performance measurement system, and high levels of manual intervention in the process. In addition, costs had increased significantly as the increasing demands for mortgage products were being met through the introduction of excessive overtime. Prior to undertaking the benchmarking exercise effectively, they had to carry out further analysis of the processes involved to obtain a better understanding of the current difficulties and requirements for performance improvement. Furthermore, carrying out this analysis facilitated the development of questionnaires and interview protocols that would be used in benchmarking and allowed better performance comparisons to be made.

The FSO identified a number of companies to benchmark including one of its sister operations and a specialist mortgage services provider. This service provider had three processing centres managing assets of £24 billion and had a number of the major UK banks as its clients. It had 15,000 different mortgage products available and assisted clients in bringing new products to market within 6 weeks, which was considerably more quickly than the FSO could achieve. The FSO adopted a three-tiered benchmarking process which identified benchmarks at the strategic, operational process and sub-process levels. These are illustrated and further described in Tables 5.5–5.7. It can be seen from Table 5.5 that the most critical strategic indicator related to speed of mortgage application processing. In order to illustrate how the benchmarking exercise was carried out, this strategic indicator is further analysed at the operational process and sub-process levels.

Key	
↑	Better than benchmarked organisation
↓	Worse than benchmarked organisation
←→	Comparable to benchmarked organisation
▓	Refers to the indicator that will be used at the next level down

Step 1: Strategic level indicators

The strategic level indicators were broadly based on the CSFs identified in Section 5.1.2. For the purposes of evaluation at this stage, the senior management team of the FSO subjectively quantified the performance of both the sister organisation and

Table 5.5   An analysis of strategic level indicators

FSO	Sister organisation	External service provider
Strategic level indicator		
The elimination of all non-value-adding processes to keeps costs low	↓ –3	↓ –4
Process mortgage applications quickly	↓ –10	↓ –10
Process mortgage applications accurately	↓ –1	↓ –1
Keep processes up to date through innovative practices	↓ –3	↓ –4

(Continued)

Table 5.5 (*Continued*)

FSO	Sister organisation	External service provider
Ensure level of resources is appropriate for volume of transactions	↓ −2	↓ −3
Ensure compliance with Financial Services Authority regulations	⟷	⟷

Table 5.6 An analysis at the operational process level

FSO	Sister organisation	External service provider
Performance measure		
Number of draw-downs	−23% ↓	−28% ↓
Application sanctioning speed	−25% ↓	−27% ↓
Speed of redemptions	−21% ↓	−20% ↓
Time spent dealing with a telephone enquiry		−27% ↓
Time spent dealing with a written enquiry		−20% ↓

Table 5.7 'Applications sanctioning speed' analysis

FSO	Sister organisation
Key performance indicator	
Quantity of applications input per day per hour	↓ −30%
Quantity of applications sanctioned per day per hour	↓ −35%
Quantity of letters of offer checking per day per hour	↓ −38%
Quantity of queries dealt with per day per hour	↓ −25%
Quantity of management interventions per day per hour	↑ 3%

external service provider by the use of a 1–10 scale, with each unit on the scale equating to 10 percentage points. For example, if one of the entities processed mortgage applications twice as quickly as the FSO, the score next to the indicator comparing its own performance against that of the entity would be −10, as it is 100% slower than the benchmarked organisation. However, it must be stressed that the senior management team acknowledged that the measurement process at this stage was fairly subjective.

Step 2: Operational process level

At the operational process level the strategic factor of 'processing mortgage applications quickly' was broken down into five process measures. Initially the only performance measure used by the FSO was 'number of draw-downs'. However, through discussions with the two benchmarking organisations, four additional measures were identified. The second and third measures came from the sister organisation as a result of the emphasis placed on mortgage turnaround time. The external service provider measured this process in the most detail. Consequently, further two measures (measures four and five) were identified by the benchmarking team. These reflected the remote nature of processing delivered by the external service provider. Both the sister organisation and external service provider were quicker in all areas that were measured as shown in Table 5.6. For example, they were 25% and 27%, quicker respectively when it came to sanctioning applications.

Step 3: The sub-process level and key performance indicators

The next stage compared how the FSO performed against key performance indicators (KPIs) at the sub-process level. The measures identified in Table 5.7 only relate to the performance measure 'applications sanctioning speed' as this was highlighted in step 2 as the poorest overall performer. For an indication of some of the other KPIs used by the FSO, refer to Table 5.10. It should also be noted that the external service provider would not divulge information on metrics at this level of detail and only those for the sister organisation are indicated. Apart from one area, quantity of management interventions per day per hour, the sister organisation outperformed the FSO, being over a third quicker in two areas.

The FSO used this analysis to further understand performance differences and how they should be addressed. In the case of its sister operations, it found that the operation performance levels were better and they also invested more in information technology to automate a number of key processes. In relation to the specialist mortgages service provider, it found that it invested a considerable amount of resource in information technology and had considerable experience in offering mortgages processing services to other leading UK FSOs. Their systems were capable of dealing with bespoke mortgage profiles, with a range of different rest periods, interest profiles, repayment plans, early settlement and flexible features. Senior management also found that the service provider had clearly defined processes and provided detailed performance measures that it was using with its major clients.

The FSO viewed benchmarking as a valuable part of the outsourcing evaluation process. However, the benchmarking exercise presented the organisation with a number of challenges. For example, as was the case with cost analysis, it was difficult to compare their internal processes with other service providers due to the idiosyncrasies and lack of clear definitions for their internal processes. Furthermore, the FSO had to rely on estimates of processing costs due to the difficulties of obtaining cost data from the service provider benchmarked. However, the financial service organisation gained a number of significant benefits from the benchmarking process. By carrying out the exercise it obtained a better understanding of internal difficulties and potential improvement strategies, as well as suitable performance metrics. For example, as demonstrated in Table 5.7, the sanctioning and checking sub-processes were particularly weak and in need of urgent improvement. Following the exercise, the FSO had a more thorough understanding of the process and an appreciation of which sub-processes affected overall performance. Furthermore, it obtained a number of important ideas for improving internal performance from the specialist mortgage service provider. It recognised the importance of having a clear understanding of the processes involved in the area of mortgages in order to measure performance. Crucially, it recognised the risks of handing over the area of mortgages to a service provider without first understanding its requirements.

5.3   Stage 3: Selecting the sourcing strategy

The preceding stages considered both the importance level of and the capability of the organisation in a process under scrutiny for outsourcing purposes. Table 5.2 summarised the results of applying the CSF method to distinguish between critical and non-critical for the four business processes of money transmission, mortgages, foreign exchange and cheque clearing. Table 5.8 summarises the results of the capability analysis for these four processes.

Based upon this analysis, the organisation identified a number of sourcing strategies for each process as shown in Figure 5.4.

A summary of the key issues associated with these sourcing strategies is presented in Table 5.9.

The following section considers the logic of each of these sourcing strategies in the quadrants presented in Figure 5.4. Detailed case illustrations are then presented for the mortgages and cheque clearing processes. In particular, these cases reveal valuable lessons for practitioners. The mortgages case illustrates how the FSO developed and improved this area of the business when it discovered that no suitable external service providers existed, whilst the cheque clearing case illustrates how the FSO outsourced this process.

Table 5.8 Process capability within the FSO

	Critical: mortgage processing	Critical: money transmission via branches	Non-critical: foreign exchange	Non-critical: cheque clearing
Capability analysis	■ Several service providers with a lower cost base and comparable levels of service were considered. However, due to lower transaction volumes, scale economies could not be achieved and the existing IT legacy systems presented integration problems. ■ Services providers could only offer standardised products. ■ Decided to transfer non-business-generating mortgage activities from the Mortgage Services Unit to internal departments that possessed required capabilities.	■ Other mainstream financial service providers would be considered as competitors and thus were not benchmarked. ■ Investigated the possibility of providing banking facilities through the post office which would provide: extended reach; longer opening hours; brand enhancement; better use of staff time through focusing on sales and relationship management.	■ The external service providers were considered more capable for the following reasons: ■ Considerably lower cost base than the bank. ■ Comparable level of service.	■ External service providers could offer significant cost reductions. ■ However, external service providers appeared to only be offering labour arbitrage and were using inferior business processes.

5.3.1 AN OVERVIEW OF THE SOURCING STRATEGIES

Quadrant 1

In this quadrant, there are external sources that are more capable than internally within the sourcing organisation for a critical process. The potential sourcing options in this quadrant are as follows:

Invest to perform internally

This option involves investing the necessary resources to bridge the disparity between the sourcing organisation and the more competent external providers of the process. The selection of this option will depend upon the following:

■ *Significance of the disparity*: If the disparity is not significant then there is the potential to invest resources in order to perform the process internally. For example, this option may be desirable in a case where the technologies involved in the process are in the embryonic stage and therefore may offer considerable scope for future growth. However, if the company's capabilities lag considerably behind the capabilities of external providers, then it may be difficult to justify a substantial investment of resources in order to match or advance upon external capabilities.

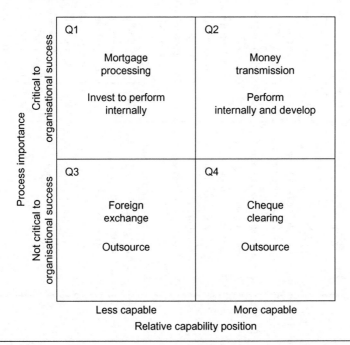

Figure 5.4 The sourcing strategies for each process at the FSO.

Table 5.9 Reasons for selection of sourcing strategies

	Critical: mortgage processing	Critical: money transmission via branches	Non-critical: foreign exchange	Non-critical: cheque clearing
Sourcing strategies	The decision to *Invest to perform internally* was influenced by (Quadrant 1):	The decision to *Perform internally and develop* was influenced by (Quadrant 2):	The decision to *Outsource* was influenced by (Quadrant 3):	The decision to *Outsource* was influenced by (Quadrant 4):
	▪ Speed up the accuracy and turnaround speed.	▪ Need to retain customer confidentiality; loss of customer contact; fear of job losses within FSO; lack of cultural fit between FSO and post office.	▪ Needed to reallocate resource from this area to more critical areas.	▪ Achieve required cost savings by establishing a new business unit with favourable terms and conditions.
	▪ Develop an area that was critical to advantage.	▪ High visibility of FSO's operations at customer interface and the need to manage risk.	▪ Supply market risk manageable due to number of available service providers.	▪ Share the costs of capital investment with partner firm.
	▪ Processes supported by SLAs.	▪ Customer relationship management of high importance to FSO.	▪ Although there was some internal resistance, the FSO believed it could manage this through staff redeployment.	▪ Retained staff could focus on more critical business areas.
	▪ Branches to concentrate on relationship development and selling of complementary mortgage products.	▪ Opportunities to focus on selling opportunities for other services.	–	▪ Potential to sell off the joint venture company in the future.

■ *Type of disparity*: The type of disparity is crucial in determining whether it is feasible to invest the necessary resources to match the superior performance of external sources. For example, if the superior cost performance of a supplier is based upon economies of scale, then it will be very difficult for the sourcing organisation to achieve such an advantage. Alternatively, analysis of the process may reveal that the disparity in performance is in an area such as quality or productivity, which can be addressed through an improvement initiative.

The *Invest to Perform Internally* option is most appropriate when the sourcing organisation is in a strong position to bridge the disparity in performance. It is important to emphasise that the organisation may have no other choice because there is considerable risk in using an external supplier for such a critical process. Also, the presence of internal constraints such as workforce resistance and the threat of industrial action may force the sourcing organisation to attempt to improve performance through an internal improvement initiative.

Outsource
This option is likely if the organisation has decided that it is not possible to attempt to bridge the disparity in performance. For example, consider an automaker that has previously designed and manufactured the engines for all its models internally. The same automaker considered engine design and manufacture to be a critical process. However, through an extensive benchmarking exercise it determined that it no longer possessed the design and manufacturing skills and resources necessary to match the performance levels achieved by other car manufacturers. Even though perceived as a critical process, it had no other choice than to source engines for a number of its models from another automaker. The importance of the process in the future should also be considered. For example, the organisation may consider outsourcing such a process, which is likely to diminish in importance in order to focus resource and effort on processes that promise to be a source of competitive differentiation in the future. Also, in certain circumstances the organisation may have no choice other than outsourcing because of internal capacity constraints. Outsourcing is most appropriate when the organisation feels the advantage the external source has in the process is too difficult to replicate.

Quadrant 2

In this quadrant, the organisation is more competent than any other potential external sources in a critical process. The most appropriate sourcing option in this quadrant is keeping the process internal. This strategy involves continuing to perform the process internally. Again, as with Quadrant 1, it is important to consider both the significance and type of disparity in performance in the process. For example, if the sourcing organisation has built up a significant performance advantage through scale economies over time, then it is going to be difficult for external sources to replicate such a capability. It is also important to assess whether the organisation can build upon the current advantage by further developing the capability in the process in order to minimise the risk of external sources matching internal performance levels. For example, a potential constraint to internal development is a lack of skilled labour or financial resources. Clearly, keeping the process internal is the most appropriate when the sourcing organisation is in a strong position to sustain its performance advantage over time. Also, it may not be possible to outsource such a process because of a lack of suppliers in the supply market that can meet the performance levels required in the process.

Quadrant 3

In this quadrant, there are external suppliers that are more capable than internally within the sourcing organisation for a process not critical to business success. These processes are suitable candidates for outsourcing. This quadrant can include many straightforward processes, products or services required by the sourcing organisation. Many companies fail to appreciate the opportunity costs of investing in processes that are not critical to business success. Furthermore, due to cultural and historical issues, there may be a prevailing view that everything can be done in-house. Attempting to perform too many processes in-house inevitably leads to a situation where no process is given the sufficient level of attention to create superior performance. Also, such an attitude may be reinforced by a culture that has failed to appreciate the capabilities of external suppliers that can perform the same processes more competently. In this quadrant, the most significant influences are the level of supply market risk and the constraints that impact upon the freedom of the organisation to outsource. For example, if there are only a limited number of capable suppliers in the supply market, the sourcing organisation may decide to continue to perform the process internally. Also, internal constraints such as the threat of industrial action may impinge upon the freedom to outsource.

Quadrant 4

In this quadrant, the organisation is more competent than potential external sources in a process that is not critical to organisational success. Although the sourcing organisation is more competent than external sources, the process is not central to competitive advantage. Therefore, the organisation should consider outsourcing such a process and focusing resources on building capabilities in processes that are more critical to the success of the organisation. However, if the organisation decides to outsource, then it will have to develop the capabilities of a supplier to the level achieved internally. There are a number ways of achieving this including a supplier development programme, through the transfer of employees and equipment to a suitable supplier or spinning off the process into a separate business. However, the organisation may decide to continue performing the process internally. For example, as with many outsourcing decisions there may be internal constraints such as workforce resistance and the costs of moving the process to an external source. Alternatively, the organisation may decide to divest itself of these types of processes in order to focus on other processes that show greater potential for future growth.

5.3.2   ILLUSTRATION: INVEST TO PERFORM INTERNALLY – THE CASE OF MORTGAGES

This illustration outlines the motives for the FSO deciding to improve the area of mortgages and keep it internal. A business transformation team (BTT) was established to investigate the feasibility of outsourcing this area. The BTT comprised senior change management staff and senior management. The Mortgage Services Unit was located at head office level and was responsible for mortgage strategy, new product development and the establishment of sales targets for each branch. In addition, it provided two critical support services: it processed mortgages sold throughout the branch network and it sanctioned large-value mortgages that were beyond the discretion of individual branches.

The BTT conducted a benchmarking review of the Mortgage Services Unit over a 3-month period. The review highlighted that mortgage volumes had increased considerably and that staff were struggling to process the volume within agreed turnaround times. The capacity problem was being tackled using expensive overtime payments but this was inadequate to meet agreed service targets. In addition, the stress on the process was creating quality problems with processing errors and inaccuracies rapidly increasing. It was also apparent that operational difficulties meant that management time was being diverted away from issues of mortgage strategy, new product development and the performance management of sales targets. If the core competencies for mortgage processing did not exist within the Mortgage Services Unit, the BTT felt that it would be more appropriate to either outsource some or all of these processes to a service provider with the necessary capabilities or to establish a shared mortgage processing centre with the sister organisation.

Despite the fact that the external service provider outperformed both the FSO and its sister organisation, the FSO had reservations about outsourcing its mortgage process. One of the reasons was that the FSO predominantly serviced a specific market niche and there was a concern that by outsourcing to an external service provider, that product ownership would be diluted. In addition, the FSO was worried that the sale of complementary products, such as insurance and loans, would be negatively affected.

As discussions with the external service provider continued, it became apparent that the customised nature of the FSOs products made it difficult for the external service provider to achieve economies of scale through process standardisation. This became apparent when a number of requests for information were received. For example, the external service provider required details such as:

- a mapping of the end-to-end process of the FSO's current mortgage processing system and an identification of the elements to be outsourced;
- the required method of interface with customers, for example e-mail, mail, telephone;
- Levels of customer satisfaction required.

Consequently, the external service provider, on receiving the information requested, suggested that some of the mortgage products could be standardised. The senior management team felt that this was unsatisfactory because it conflicted with the FSO's market positioning strategy. The external service provider was removed from the evaluation process, leaving the sister organisation for benchmarking purposes.

With regard to the proposed shared services centre with the sister organisation there were a number of strategic issues, which had not been considered during the benchmarking phase. It should be noted that the sister organisation was located outside the UK. Senior management raised the issue of financial and legal regulations related to different European jurisdictions. These regulations affected how the mortgage application process had to be performed and therefore it could not have been integrated into the current systems of the sister organisation. In addition, from the cost analysis (presented in Section 5.2.1) it can be seen that the sister organisation has faster turnaround times in terms of mortgage completions. One of the main reasons for this is the high degree of automation. These systems had been in place for in excess of 5 years and there was a concern from an information systems perspective that there would be great difficulty in integrating the legacy systems of the sister organisation with new technology in the FSO. Finally, the FSO has a non-redundancy policy; this means that any members of staff whose job was affected by the establishment of a shared services centre could not be laid off. They would need to be retrained to work in another area of the organisation. This meant that any immediate cost savings would not be recognised and that costs would actually increase, as the FSO would be paying for both the outsourced operation and the salaries of staff that were adding little or no value in the short term. Consequently, the BTT decided that it would be more appropriate to perform mortgage processing internally and develop them.

The internal investment involved undertaking a major business improvement exercise. The BTT restructured the area of mortgages, which involved reducing the headcount through the re-design of operational processes. Senior management believed that such a reorganisation would enable the retained staff to concentrate their efforts on mortgage strategy, regulation and sales. Mortgage processing and mortgage fulfilment processes would be transferred to the Branch Services Unit where they could be managed alongside existing back-office processes that were performed on behalf of the branch network. The preparation of mortgage deeds was relocated to the Central Securities Unit where existing expertise in securities functions was expanded to incorporate mortgage deeds. The BTT decided that the mortgage sanctioning and staff business teams be transferred from the Mortgage Services Unit into the Large-Value Credit Sanctioning Unit where expertise in large-value lending existed.

Investing in and keeping mortgages internally had major implications for IT and facilities requirements. In addition, the entire project had to be carried out without any adverse operational impacts on the business. Consequently, the BTT established a number of teams. An executive communication team was formed comprising directors and senior management executives from each impacted area. Three working groups, chaired by the management of the Branch Services Unit, Large-Value Credit Sanctioning Unit and the Securities Unit respectively, were formed to identify and manage each work stream. Each working group comprised members from the Mortgage Services Unit, the selected internal department and representatives from the IT and facilities departments. In addition, a representative from the Internal Compliance Unit was selected for each working group because mortgages are regulated products. Key targets and milestones were focused around staff transfers, facilities and IT reorganisations. Individual tasks were identified and project plans established to monitor tasks and ensure all were agreed prior to the move. A Steering Group was also set up and chaired by the leader of the BTT. This group met fortnightly to monitor progress from the working groups and address or escalate issues to the executive communication team. The management of each internal team had been tasked with maximising efficiency and effectiveness. The executive communication team and the steering group continued to meet after the improvement exercise had been implemented in order to address any ongoing issues of concern. SLAs were then developed between the restructured Mortgage Services Unit and the relevant internal departments. Sample metrics from the three SLAs developed are detailed in Table 5.10.

5.3.3 ILLUSTRATION: OUTSOURCING CHEQUE CLEARING AT THE FSO

This case outlines the motives for the FSO outsourcing the cheque clearing process. The cheque clearing process involves transferring cheques between bank branches and different banking organisations in order to exchange funds. A major driver for considering outsourcing had come from corporate level. The need to reduce the costs of routine transactions had been identified as a CSF. The process of clearing cheques was one such routine transaction. Although this process had to be performed well, it

Table 5.10 Sample service levels

Branch Services Unit – mortgage processing

Activity	KPI measurement (per person)
Application input	Applications per day
Regulation/Quality control	Applications per hour
Letter of offer checking	Letters per day
Administration assistant	Per volumes
Post	Pieces per day
Regulation/Operational checking	Quantity per hour
Letter of offer checking	Quantity per day
Post	Items per day
Redemption quotes	Quantity per hour
Redemption (full settlements/capital reductions)	Quantity per hour
Central Securities Unit – mortgage deeds	
Deeds in	Quantity per hour
Deeds out	Quantity per hour
Assignment of policy post	Items per hour
Vacation of deeds	Quantity per hour
Queries and post	Volume and management interaction
Large-Value Credit Sanctioning Unit – mortgage sanctioning	
Application sanctioning	Quantity per hour

was not critical to competitive advantage. Whilst the cheque clearing process involves significant investments in technology, the capability of efficient cheque clearing does not impact significantly on the ability of the FSO to achieve competitive advantage. The supporting IT infrastructure for cheque clearing in the case study organisation was old and required significant capital investment in order to generate process improvements. Such an investment would have contradicted the organisation's strategic objective to reduce its cost base. The sub-process transactions were high volume and repetitive in nature and were particularly labour intensive. Another challenge was the use of experienced banking personnel to perform the transactional processing activities associated with the cheque clearing process. However, the advantage of using such staff was that the processes were well understood and stable.

The FSO recognised the importance of improving the capability of their staff particularly in areas of customer service. It was hoped that experienced staff could be diverted away from simple transaction processing into higher value-generating activities. Whilst the case study organisation was aware that an emerging cost reduction initiative used by other banks was to use offshore services for cheque clearing, they felt that the offshore provision of cheque clearing was not a mature business. Consequently they did not feel sufficiently confident to allow a vendor to take responsibility for the operational management of cheque clearing. Poor process performance times in clearing cheques would have resulted in a significant negative impact on the organisation's profitability and operating capability. Therefore, the challenge was to reduce the costs of transactional processing without significant capital investment or the loss of operational control.

As part of the outsourcing evaluation process, the FSO carried out an analysis of its performance and found that it had strong internal capabilities in this area. In particular, it found that processing times in the cheque clearing process were comparable if not better than other companies that it considered. The FSO approached one of its competitors with a view to establishing an independent outsourcing services provider for cheque clearing processes. Following lengthy negotiations, both organisations agreed to establish a joint venture that would provide cheque clearing services. As well as offering cheque clearing services to the parent companies, the service provider could offer these services to other FSOs in order to further grow its business. Through further developing its business, it was anticipated that the service provider would realise greater cost reductions and economies of scale through processing cheques for other financial service organisations. For the purposes of clarity in this report, the case study organisation will be referred to as FSO 1 and the joint venture partner as FSO 2.

FSO 1: Objectives of outsourcing cheque clearing

The FSO identified four objectives for outsourcing its cheque clearing processes:

- improved customer services;
- reduction in operational risk;
- reduced investment;
- reduced operational costs.

It was a key objective to re-deploy experienced banking staff involved in cheque clearing into higher value adding activities. It was envisaged that their banking experience could be effectively deployed through developing workflows for improved processes associated with customer account administration and customer service or the management of such processes; alternatively they could be moved into business development roles within the bank. Historically, the cheque clearing process had the potential to reduce customer service and profitability if performed inefficiently. It was felt that handing over the responsibility for cheque clearing to an organisation for which this process was their only responsibility would reduce the operational risks. Another objective was to reduce investment. The expenses associated with capital investment in IT hardware and software could be reduced, as the outsourced provider would be able to spread the costs of such investments over a much larger volume of transactions. The operational costs for the clearing of cheques could be reduced in a number of ways. First, the provider would be realising economies of scale. In addition, their staff could be employed at lower labour rates than were being paid to experienced banking employees and without providing the labour benefits associated with union membership that has been typical in the banking industry.

5.4 Stage 4: Implementing and managing the outsourcing arrangement

This stage sets out the issues that have to be considered when implementing and managing the outsourcing relationship. The management of the outsourcing relationship is being increasingly considered in the academic literature (DiRomualdo and Gurbaxani, 1998; Dyer and Singh, 1998; Lorenzoni and Lipparini, 1999; Helper et al., 2000; Poppo and Zenger, 2002; Ho et al., 2003; Langfield-Smith and Smith, 2003; Webb and Laborde, 2005).

The first stage is concerned with dealing with the contracting issues and will address factors such as the SLA, transfer of staff and assets, price and payment terms, liability and contract termination. Once the contract has been negotiated and drawn up, the client then establishes and manages the relationship with the supplier. The people responsible for managing the relationship must have the necessary skills and experience to ensure the relationship meets the objectives of the outsourcing strategy. Evaluation of relationship performance will be carried out on an ongoing basis addressing a number of issues including supplier performance, strength of the relationship and the level of dependency on the supplier. This evaluation serves as a framework for action, which can involve maintaining the relationship at its current level, further developing the relationship or discontinuing or reducing the scope of the relationship.

5.4.1 CONTRACTING ISSUES

The importance of contracting issues in outsourcing has been established in the literature (Gainey and Klaas, 2003; Narayanan and Raman, 2004; Spekman and Davis, 2004; Anderson and Dekker, 2005; Mani et al., 2005). It is important to establish clear objectives for outsourcing. These outsourcing objectives can also be used as a basis for drawing up a contract for the outsourcing process. A well-designed contract can allow for most future contingencies and how these contingencies should be dealt with. It is better to have a clear idea of what is required in order to avoid any potential gaps in the contract. The type of process being sourced and the level of risk in the supply market will influence the design of the contract. For example, in the case of a straightforward process with a significant number of suppliers in the supply market, the objectives of outsourcing the process and requirements of the supplier are well defined. Alternatively, if there is uncertainty about the requirements the contract must be designed to reflect this uncertainty. The performance measures incorporated into the contract – often via the SLA – must reflect the objectives of the outsourcing strategy. For example, it is unlikely that a contract which focuses primarily on price reductions will lead to the development of a relationship that is designed to foster and encourage inter-firm innovation.

Although the SLA is an important element of outsourcing arrangements, there are potential problems with implementation. The major reasons for the failure of SLAs include poor measurements, inadequate definitions and a lack of the required resource commitment. The SLA requires a significant resource commitment on the part of the customer. For example, the customer has to agree to support the objectives of the SLA through the provision of accurate forecasts, attainable deadlines and realistic cost targets. The nature of the client–supplier relationship will influence the level of resource that should be committed to managing the SLA. Owing to the contractual nature of the SLA, it is important to employ it in the proper context. For example, in the context of a cost-focused transactional client–supplier relationship, contractual provisions can be included to penalise the supplier financially if at any time the supplier fails to deliver the level of service required. Alternatively, in the case of a close collaborative relationship rigid adherence to the contract can damage a relationship, which may be attempting to foster innovation and joint improvement. In this case, it is more appropriate to use the SLA as a guide in creating a service management ethos and aligning the relationship to the objectives of outsourcing. Also, evaluation of supplier performance will focus more on intangible factors that contribute to the improvement of the quality of service and the health of the customer–supplier relationship.

5.4.2 ILLUSTRATION: IMPLEMENTING AND MANAGING THE OUTSOURCING OF CHEQUE CLEARING

This illustration outlines how the outsourcing of cheque clearing was implemented. Particular emphasis is given to issue of performance measurement. FSO 1 had established that cheque clearing was not critical to organisational success and that their internal capability was strong when compared with external providers and competitors. Referring to the outsourcing framework in Figure 5.4, this presented

Table 5.11 The implementation preparation schedule

	February				March				April				May				June		
Project definition	▓	▓																	
Identifying customer requirements	▓	▓	▓	▓	▓														
Consideration of IT architecture					▓	▓													
Functional specifications									▓	▓	▓	▓	▓						
Technical systems									▓	▓	▓	▓	▓						
Supplier evaluation				▓	▓	▓	▓	▓	▓	▓									
Completing business case				▓	▓	▓	▓	▓	▓	▓									
Establishing a steering committee			▓													▓			
Design reviews																	▓		

the FSO with a choice between keeping the process internal and outsourcing it. In the end, FSO 1 established a joint venture with a competitor FSO 2 for the provision of cheque clearing processes for the international network of banks operated by both institutions. The scope of engagement involved all the processes associated with the clearing of cheques including out-clearing, debit in-clearing, credit referencing and settlement.

Planning for implementation

Table 5.11 illustrates the schedule used by FSO 1 when preparing to outsource the cheque clearing process. This period of preparation lasted for 5 months and was performed in collaboration with an independent project manager.

The first month was spent establishing the requirements of the cheque clearing process to be provided by an external provider. A project team of six people was established to work on this task. This was a cross-functional team comprising senior management, cheque clearing staff and other stakeholders. A series of in-depth interviews was conducted with bank stakeholders to agree on the key principles of the outsourcing arrangement. These were high-level discussions at this stage and not concerned with detailed requirements. The negotiation phase lasted for about 14 weeks. A project manager was recruited and a number of work streams were created for the project as illustrated in Table 5.12.

The first six weeks involved largely preparative work and involved the project team giving consideration to customer requirements, IT architecture, functional specifications, etc. It was necessary to delve into more detail into the requirements and as a result of this detailed analysis the contract was developed.

Developing the governance contract

The primary objective of outsourcing cheque clearing was cost reduction. The process was deemed to be non-core and transactional in nature. The governance contract included sections on the transfer of staff and assets, price and payment terms,

Table 5.12 Project work streams

Work stream	Responsibility
Software applications development	Project manager
IT transmission requirements	Project manager, FSO 1 and FSO 2
Operations	FSO 1 and FSO 2
Testing and Training	FSO 1 and FSO 2
Implementation	Project manager, FSO 1 and FSO 2
Infrastructure requirements	Project manager, FSO 1 and FSO 2
Premises	FSO 1
Staff transition	FSO 2
Business operations design	FSO 1 and FSO 2

penalties, liability and contract termination and service levels. Service levels were defined in an SLA. Development of an SLA involved an appreciation of both business and operations strategy, business process analysis and performance management and measurement. Concentrating on business strategy forced the organisation to consider which factors are critical to its competitive position. These factors translated into operational performance measures such as quality, responsiveness and cost. Performance management relied on the use of relevant indicator metrics across these operational elements to influence the behaviour of the service provider.

For the FSO the development of performance metrics for the SLA involved undertaking detailed process analysis and workflow mapping to establish the tasks that are critical to performing the process and associated levels of performance. This involved identifying and defining the distinctive tasks, choosing the ideal sequence that tasks would follow and determining who would be responsible for performing them. Such a process analysis exercise involved the development of graphical workflow diagrams indicating the flow of materials, people and information through the process. The workflow influenced the selection of process metrics. As well as establishing what should be measured, it was necessary to consider the required frequency of measurement, the required frequency of reporting and by what method the measurement would take place. In the case of cheque clearing, the FSO subdivided the process into a number of sub-processes: *out-clearing*, *debit in-clearing*, *encoding* and *credit referencing/settlement*. A detailed analysis of each sub-process was performed using workflow techniques. Appendix 2 illustrates a workflow chart for the *encoding* sub-process.

This analysis highlighted the key tasks involved and influenced the development of the process metrics that were used in the SLA. Employing this approach allowed the organisation to concentrate on the procedures and metrics that would allow the service provider to better understand and meet its requirements. A detailed SLA was developed as a result of this approach. The process-specific metrics focused primarily on operational objectives including quality and responsiveness. Historically, FSO 1 and FSO 2 had differing levels of turnaround performance regarding their cheque clearing processes with FSO 1 achieving shorter turnaround times than FSO 2. It was a medium-term goal that FSO 2 would improve their turnaround performance but the immediate objective for the external service provider was that traditional service levels for FSO 1 and FSO 2 would be maintained. To facilitate this, the KPIs for service were prioritised by each FSO. KPIs were developed under the criteria of quality and timeliness. The contract was primarily fixed cost, which meant that KPIs regarding cost did not need to feature in the SLA. It was agreed that any changes in the scope of the agreement would be charged for by the provider. Appendix 3 illustrates the complexity of the SLA by providing a sample of the KPI metrics associated with quality and timeliness for each of the cheque clearing sub-processes. The required service levels were stepped by time; that is performance improvement targets were built into the SLA. Penalty clauses were agreed for non-achievement of service.

Making the transition

The commencement of the joint venture necessitated the reengineering of the cheque clearing process. The two organisations had been using different approaches to cheque clearing and neither organisation had a standardised process for use across business units or national boundaries. The joint venture organisation sought the deployment of best practices and process workflows to achieve best-in-class productivity and delivery. This transitional stage involved detailed process, workflow and document analyses over a 2-month period. Sorting machine capacities were verified so that increased processing volumes would be handled. In addition, a series of process metrics were collected. The FSO created a risk register to help manage the transition process as illustrated in Table 5.13. Developing a risk register forced the FSO to develop contingencies for the transition. A steering group met weekly to monitor and evaluate progress and to take corrective action as necessary.

At this same time, there was no site or resources for the supplier organisation. An investigation of cheque volumes and delivery patterns was performed as part of the location analysis. Consideration was given to courier delivery patterns and to traffic congestion for deliveries affecting turnaround times. The number of staff that would be needed to run the new facility had to be calculated together with the physical resources such as sorting machines that are required. HR issues including staffing,

Table 5.13   Risk register

	Likelihood	Impact
Branch capture system not rolled out on time.	Medium	High
Plan is unable to resolve resource smoothing issues.	Medium	High
Dependent applications in either bank may change, for example branch capture system.	Medium	High
Project organisation structure not changed to reflect the business requirements and cause delays.	Low	High
Resources available are not correctly skilled to complete tasks.	Medium	High
Third party costs are unacceptably high weakening the business case.	High	High
The number of changes is high causing additional costs and delays.	Medium	Medium
Development is not to specification and contains errors.	Medium	High
Budget overruns with regard to changes, business issues, internal dependencies, technical issues, etc.	Medium	High
Joint venture not able to obtain exempt supplier status for VAT.	Medium	Medium
Remuneration structure cannot be agreed.	Low	Medium

organisation structure, salaries and job descriptions were also established during this period. From an operational perspective, office plans and layouts were designed.

The credit side of cheque clearing went live in July and was fully operational by September of the same year. Employees were recruited and trained in how to use the sorting technology during this time. Out-clearing which had previously been branch-based also went live in September. The 'go-live' was staggered over a period of 2 months so that the project team was confident of its reliability. During this period, a contingency machine was still running in the FSO. Two weeks after 'go-live', there was about 10% of the process active on the new machine. The next 2 weeks saw a rapid ramp-up so that 50% was active on the new machine after

4 weeks. All of the process was transferred to the new technology after 8 weeks. From this point, the provision of the cheque clearing process was the sole responsibility of the external service provider.

However, following the transition, the external provider had difficulties with processing cheques from FSO 2. This resulted from FSO 2 changing their internal bank remittance process without consulting or informing the service provider of cheque clearing. The bank remittance process feeds the cheque clearing process. Changes to bank remittance meant that the cheque clearing software did not receive the information in the correct order causing the system to crash. Consequently, the turnaround time targets could not be met for this KPI. Whilst this may not have been a critical SLA metric, it resulted in additional costs due to the requirement to use overtime labour. This had important implications for relationship management. The problem highlighted that the training for retained staff in processes linked to cheque clearing had not been adequate. There was also a lack of IT resource or capability at FSO 2, which meant that the processes feeding cheque clearing could not be managed as effectively. A further problem concerned the quality of paper that FSO 2 was using to transfer the cheque clearing details to the mainframe. The paper quality was poor, which caused the IT hardware to reject a number of cheques for processing. The reject rate was running at 19%. Consequently it was not possible for the provider to meet quality targets associated with the SLA.

5.4.3 MANAGING THE RELATIONSHIP

The direction and management of the relationship will be influenced by the objectives of the outsourcing strategy. It is critical that both the outsourcing organisation and the outsourcing provider have the necessary skills and resources to manage the interaction process at the operational level. The interaction process will differ considerably depending upon the type of relationship adopted. For example, managing a close collaborative relationship requires substantial investments from both organisations. However, if the focus of the outsourcing arrangement is on transactional processes, the relationship is likely to be more adversarial. The relationship interface is likely to be confined to the account manager and the outsourcing manager, for example often the Chief Financial Officer with limited involvement from the strategic level of each business. The interaction patterns between the relevant participants at the client–supplier interface are critical in ensuring the development of a close collaborative relationship. This will involve a significant resource commitment and will also rely on input from senior management at various stages in the development of the relationship. In the early stages of the relationship interaction is important to enable a good rapport to develop between the people responsible for managing the relationship. Meetings between the top management of both the outsourcing organisation and the supplier will take place to demonstrate the high level of commitment to the relationship. Visits by the personnel of both the client and the supplier to their respective sites are essential in creating a mutual understanding of each party's needs and capabilities. Face-to-face interaction is the most successful means of understanding the needs of both parties. To this end it can be a valuable investment by the outsourcing supplier to install a relationship manager at the client site particularly during the transition phase.

Relationship performance evaluation

The importance of relationship management in the context of outsourcing has already been emphasised. Much of the risk associated with outsourcing arises from the failure of suppliers to deliver and meet the requirements of the client. In order to reduce these risks and pre-empt supplier failure, the outsourcing organisation must have a formal mechanism to determine whether the supplier is meeting the performance levels set and whether the objectives in its approach to relationship management are being achieved. There are a number of aspects that should be considered in this evaluation including supplier performance and the strength of the relationship.

Service provider performance

Evaluation of service provider performance is concerned with determining whether the supplier is delivering to the required standards during the contract. This analysis will focus on performance metrics related to quality, delivery, service and ability to reduce costs. Having an effective mechanism of evaluating supplier performance can also serve as basis for comparing performance levels with that of other potential suppliers in the supply market. The approach to evaluation will depend upon the nature of the relationship. In the case of a cost-focused transactional relationship, the client will focus on measuring the performance of the supplier quantitatively along a number of criteria including price, quality and delivery. As with the supplier selection decision, the dominant criteria in the evaluation will be price and cost reduction. The focus is on inspecting the outcomes of the process rather than attempt to diagnose the causes of poor performance. The responsibility for performance rests solely with the supplier with little or no assistance provided from the client to resolve problems.

In the case of a collaborative relationship, the approach to evaluation differs considerably. The importance of measuring and monitoring performance in a collaborative relationship is emphasised by the increased dependency between the client and the supplier. The evaluation of performance is a joint process with both the client and the supplier attempting to identify and deal with the causes of poor performance in any areas. Therefore, as both the client and the supplier are responsible for the success of the relationship, the focus is on improvement. This focus on improvement not only centres on cost reduction but also can encompass any area of operations.

There is also an onus on the client to achieve improvements. The client may attempt to achieve improvements that can assist the supplier in meeting the required performance levels. Therefore, both the client and the supplier must be aware of each other's expectations of performance. The development of close collaborative relationships will involve the client and the supplier working jointly over the long term to improve performance levels and meet each other's expectations.

The strength of the relationship

As well as evaluating supplier performance, the nature of the relationship with the supplier must be evaluated. Evaluation of the strength of the supply relationship will be guided by the initial objectives established for the outsourcing process. This evaluation is most appropriate in the context of collaborative relationships. For example, monitoring the strength of a close collaborative relationship will involve analysing the presence of intangible factors such as joint problem solving, high levels of information exchange and top management commitment from both the client and the supplier. Table 5.14 provides a useful categorisation of the factors that describe the strength of the relationship.

The strength of the relationship describes the factors that create bonds between the client and the supplier. The economic factors describe the level of dependency of the supplier on the client. Exit costs relate to the level of investments made by the supplier that are specific to the needs of the client. High exit costs limit the ability of the supplier to transfer these investments to other clients. For example, extensive customisation of software relating to business processes, location of operations, etc. will result in high exit costs. The characteristics of the relationship describe the factors that create stronger bonds between the client and the supplier. For example, a high frequency and wide range of information exchange between the participants at the client–supplier interface can facilitate the development of a strong relationship. Also, these bonds will be further strengthened if these exchange mechanisms have been developed over a long period of time. Co-operation between the client and the supplier indicates the level of collaboration at various levels at the client–supplier interface. This can also include co-operation in areas of integrating systems to facilitate greater transparency between the client and the supplier. Distance between the client and the supplier is composed of five factors (Ford, 1984). Social distance relates to the familiarity of the individuals who manage the relationship in both the client and the supplier. Cultural distance refers to the differences between the norms and values of the client and the supplier. Technological distance relates to the differences between process technologies of the client and the supplier. Time distance describes the time between making a change request and the completion of the service involved. Finally, geographical distance refers to the physical distance between the client and the supplier.

Table 5.14 Factors indicating the strength of the relationship

Factor

Economic factors
1. Financial value of the outsourcing contract as a percentage of supplier turnover
2. Strategic importance of the client to the supplier
3. Exit costs

Characteristics of the relationship
1. Types of information exchanged
2. Willingness to share information
3. Frequency of communication
4. Level and number of personal contacts
5. Duration of the relationship

Co-operation between client and supplier
1. Co-operation in areas such as business process improvement and innovation
2. Willingness to integrate systems
3. Integration of management

Distance between the client and the supplier
1. Social distance
2. Cultural distance
3. Technological distance
4. Time distance
5. Geographical distance

Source: Adapted from Olsen and Ellram (1997) and Kannan and Tan (2002).

5.4.4 ILLUSTRATION: MANAGING THE CHEQUE CLEARING RELATIONSHIP

The nature of this outsourcing arrangement was the provision of transactional processes deemed non-core to the FSO. The nature of the relationship was largely cost driven. As part of the outsourcing transition, two senior members of staff from FSO were seconded on site to manage the transition process of implementation and to provide training for the newly recruited workforce. These included a manager with over 20 years of banking experience who was on site with the outsourcing provider for a period of 9 months. The second FSO employee was on site for 7 months. Such a commitment had not been planned for when the business case had been developed. This investment helped to develop a strong understanding by the supplier of the performance levels that had to be achieved. Although FSO 2 had been responsible for staff transition, they did not spend time at the supplier premises. In addition, the supplier worked from dedicated premises and did not spend time on site at both the FSOs. This meant that no strong relationships were built up with the personnel working in the related business processes that impacted upon service levels and performance in the contract. Likewise once the FSO managers had returned to their organisations, there was no further input to the business processes associated with cheque clearing. There was no focus on continuous improvement or any motivation to do so. Such elements are consistent with a cost-focused transactional relationship. Both FSOs stated that they considered the outsourcing provider to be like any external service provider. However, such an approach to relationship management did have a negative impact on performance outcomes.

In relation to performance measurement in the outsourcing relationship, the contract and SLA played a pivotal role for the FSO. In the case of cheque clearing, performance management involved a resource commitment on the part of both the FSO and the service provider. The senior management team met monthly to assess the performance of the outsourced cheque clearing service. There were a number of parties involved in managing this process. In the FSO, a relationship promoter was appointed; the senior management team was involved primarily in the measurement and examination of the performance of the service provider against the agreed service levels. The relationship promoter along with the internal users of the cheque clearing process in the FSO was involved in creating an environment in which the agreed service levels could be met. Furthermore, the relationship promoter was responsible for dealing with changes in the FSO's requirements and implementing contract variations. The service delivery manager in the supplier organisation was responsible for resolving operational problems and managing routine changes in accordance with the SLA. This manager liaised directly with the relationship promoter in the FSO in order to address any performance problems.

The transactional nature of the arrangement meant that there was little co-operation and coordination between the client and the service provider. However, this led to a number of performance problems especially when the service provider was tasked with working to more challenging targets. The experiences of the FSO here suggest that collaboration is more likely to occur if improvement of process performance is required. Indeed it would seem that is more likely to occur as the duration of the outsourcing relationship lengthens. Appendix 4 shows how performance changed over time by illustrating the performance of the debit in-clearing sub-process over the first 3 years of the outsourcing arrangement.

Performance for the first 9 months was supported by the presence of experienced banking personnel. After that period, the responsibility for the performance outcomes transferred to the service delivery manager in the service provider. Performance suffered at this stage and a number of factors contributed to this outcome. As a result of the service provider being off-site, it was not possible to develop strong personal relationships with the staff in related processes within the two FSOs. It was clear that the staff in FSO 2 were unaware of the effect of their actions on the perform-ance targets for the outsourcing provider. For example, the quality of paper being used by FSO 2 to transfer the cheque clearing details to the mainframe was poor and caused the IT hardware to reject cheques for processing. Quality performance lagged behind targets for some time and penalty clauses in the contract were acted upon. It was only when the parties involved agreed to set aside the contract and attempt to address the problem collectively that progress began to be made.

Lack of collaboration in the initial stages resulted in FSO 2 changing their inter-nal bank remittance process without consulting or informing the service provider of cheque clearing which resulted in the cheque clearing software not receiving the information in the correct order, and crashing. This affected turnaround time targets and created additional costs. Performance in the area of timeliness was high in the initial stages of the outsourcing agreement. This was helped by the fact that FSO 2 accepted a slower rate of cheque processing than FSO 1. Using a combination of job prioritisation and overtime, it was possible for the provider to reach the targets set in the SLA. However, after about 15 months, the FSO 2 cheque processing tar-gets stepped up to match those of their joint venture partner FSO 1. The outsourcing provider was unable to meet this new target and it took time for the organisations to accept that they would have to get more involved with the service provider in order to make improvements.

For much of the duration of the outsourcing agreement, the service provider made use of overtime working to meet the quality and timeliness metrics in the SLA. This meant that the provider was unable to meet their internal cost targets for profitabil-ity. As the agreement was largely a fixed-price one, there was no motivation for the FSOs to address the problems of cost. However, as the organisations started to collaborate more to address the problems associated with quality and timeliness, the service provider was able to make the efficiencies necessary to reduce the over-time working. The parties have realised that although the outsourcing arrangement is for the provision of non-core processes, some collaborative working is neces-sary. Indeed, the most recent case of collaboration has involved the parties coming together to agree procedural modifications to comply with changes to cheque clear-ing recommended by the Office of Fair Trading (OFT). The Payment System Task Force established by the OFT in 2004 recommended changes to the cheque clearing cycle which were agreed by the Chancellor of the Exchequer in November 2006 and become effective from November 2007. Maximum times have now been estab-lished for the cheque clearing cycle. These recommendations have reduced the time available to complete the cheque clearing cycle and have had a knock on effect on the KPIs in the SLA with the external provider.

Chapter 6

Evaluation of the Outsourcing Framework

The aim of this research was to develop a framework, which incorporates performance measures that can be used in the outsourcing process. The outsourcing framework developed as part of this research integrates a number of important performance management considerations developing CFSs, analysing internal performance prior to outsourcing, cost analysis, benchmarking, and performance measurement and management throughout the outsourcing relationship. This framework provides a structured approach for considering these important elements of outsourcing. Table 6.1 summarises the key performance management issues associated with the outsourcing framework.

Table 6.1   Performance management issues and the outsourcing framework

Performance management issues

- ■ Does achieving superior performance levels in the process enable your organisation achieve a competitive advantage within the industry?
- ■ Will investing additional resource in the process allow your organisation to achieve a competitive advantage?
- ■ Is it likely that senior management will commit additional internal resource to achieving superior performance levels in the process?
- ■ Is it difficult to understand how your organisation or a service provider/ competitor achieves superior performance levels in the process?
- ■ Do superior performance levels in the process rapidly decline without considerable investments of time and money?
- ■ How critical are the results of the outsourced process to the execution of one or more outsourced processes?
- ■ Is it possible to establish clear performance levels for service providers in the process, for example, in terms of quantity, quality and timeliness of output?
- ■ Is it possible to negotiate a contract that clearly specifies the standards of service provider performance required and the means of evaluation?
- ■ Is it possible to establish clear written rules and procedures to enable the service provider to perform the process?

Application of the framework at the FSO has identified the benefits and challenges of applying such a framework in practice. Furthermore, these findings have important implications for organisations integrating performance management into the outsourcing process. These implications are now explored.

Many organisations find it difficult to distinguish between core processes that should be performed internally and non-core process that are suitable for outsourcing. The outsourcing framework in this research employed the CSF method to assist with this analysis. The FSO studied found the identification of CSFs to be a valuable exercise. In determining CSFs, the FSO was influenced by the needs of its customers and maintaining its competitive position, which were central elements of its business strategy. However, it found determining the importance level of processes to be a considerable challenge. The workshops conducted stimulated considerable debate and highlighted difficulties amongst management on the importance level of processes in relation to the CSFs. For example, the FSO had to rethink some definitions of its current processes in order to create greater clarity. However, through using the CSF methodology in the context of outsourcing, the organisation reached consensus and made a judgement, albeit subjective, on critical and non-critical processes.

A major part of the analysis in the outsourcing framework involves assessing the relative performance capability in a process in relation to external service providers. This was found to be a challenging exercise for the FSO. Prior to application of the outsourcing framework, existing performance measures used by the FSO were found to be inadequate for analysing process capability. Much of the performance management was undertaken at the strategic level with insufficient emphasis being placed at the process level. Developing performance measures for processes prior to outsourcing is a key aspect of effective outsourcing. In particular, where organisations outsource processes without developing performance measures they have no way of knowing whether service providers are executing processes better or worse than internal departments. As part of the analysis for this stage of the framework, the FSO carried out in-depth analysis of internal processes and also benchmarked service providers. Although process analysis is time consuming and difficult as evidenced by the experiences of the FSO, it is an important element of outsourcing in a number of areas:

- analysing and determining causes of poor performance;
- understanding internal and external process inter-dependencies;
- understanding and determining process requirements;
- determining performance measures for the contract and SLA;
- determining required service provider capabilities;
- clearly communicating requirements to the service provider;
- selecting the most appropriate service provider relationship.

An interesting finding from the experiences of the FSO was the impact that the analysis of existing internal processes and service provider capabilities had upon the outsourcing process. The analysis had a significant impact upon the outsourcing of mortgages. In-depth analysis of existing processes internally in this area alerted the company to the need for significant redesign of existing processes. If it had based its decision on the analysis of service providers alone, it may have outsourced mortgages and created a situation in which the service provider was unable to meet its requirements. This is a common problem in outsourcing as organisations tend to be taken in by overzealous service providers exaggerating their capabilities in order to secure business.

A significant benefit of the FSO benchmarking its performance and capabilities with that of external service providers was that it enabled the organisation to identify and develop performance metrics for processes, which could be used to assess performance for an outsourced process or one retained in-house. For example, when it benchmarked its capabilities in mortgage processing with that of a specialist mortgage processing service provider it identified suitable measures for assessing performance in this area. Assessments of organisational capability relative to external service providers raised the importance of service provider capabilities considerations in other areas of outsourcing. An outcome of analysing external service providers was that it created a greater awareness of service provider capabilities, which in particular alerted the FSO to potential opportunities for outsourcing additional processes in the future.

In relation to cost analysis in the outsourcing decision, the FSO compared its costs with those of its sister organisation which proved to be beneficial from a number of perspectives: first, it highlighted areas where the sister organisation was keeping its costs much lower; second, it showed the FSO that the cost differences were mainly due to inefficient work practices rather than a lack of productivity by its own work force and third, it set a benchmark which the FSO could subsequently aim for when it came to measures such as overall cost per mortgage and staff cost per mortgage. Adhering strictly to the logic of the outsourcing framework, cost analysis in the outsourcing decision should involve comparing the costs of sourcing a process internally or from an external service provider. However, this is a major challenge for a number of reasons as evidenced by the findings here. Unless the sourcing organisation and the service provider have standardised processes, it is not possible to derive fully objective cost comparisons. For example, when the FSO was comparing costs with that of an external service provider it was unable to gain any accurate cost data, and when it was comparing itself to its sister organisation, fixed costs such as the much higher price of accommodation in the latter's home country were not taken into consideration. Another limitation involves the amount of cost data that service providers are willing to provide due to the risks of competitors accessing such sensitive data. However, the major benefit of analysing the costs associated with a process is that it provides a mechanism for identifying how costs can be reduced via process redesign internally or outsourcing to a service provider. Nevertheless, prior to making the outsourcing decision it is essential that only relevant costs, that is those that are affected by the decision, are taken into consideration.

Linking the dimensions of process importance and performance capability to provide potential sourcing strategies is a central element of the outsourcing framework. Assessing process importance and performance capability was considered a valuable tool for discussion and provided a language that could be understood in a practical context. One of the major reasons for identifying critical and non-critical processes in the context of outsourcing was to ensure that processes that were deemed crucial to the overall performance and success of the organisation were not lost to service providers. However, interviews with management revealed other related benefits in assessing process importance. It served as a valuable basis for prioritising which processes required immediate attention through either internal improvement or outsourcing. Furthermore, it was a valuable indicator of the likely impact of service provider failure in the case of a process that was considered suitable for outsourcing. Consideration of the sustainability of any superior performance position in a process was a key part of the analysis for the FSO. Placing the analysis in this context allowed the organisation to consider the implications for the strategic development of the organisation and resource allocation. For example, it believed it would have to allocate internal investment into the money transmission process in order to improve its performance and therefore justify keeping it internally. The concept of achieving high levels of performance on an ongoing basis – either through performing the process internally or outsourcing – was an important consideration in satisfying the strategic priorities of the FSO.

The experiences of the organisation that participated in this research support the view in the literature that detailed contracts and collaboration are complementary in outsourcing arrangements (Poppo and Zenger, 2002; McIvor, 2008). Drafting a tight contract can act as an important complement to building an ethos of collaboration and problem solving in the relationship. It is often assumed that partnering and collaboration alone can deal with any difficulties in the relationship. However, a carefully drafted contract can serve as an impetus for action and improvement. In particular, the contract allows the buyer and supplier to establish expectations and make commitments to short-term objectives. Furthermore, it is important to place the role of collaboration in outsourcing relationships. There is much rhetoric in the academic literature and practice in relation to collaboration and partnerships in outsourcing relationships. For example, some argue that partnerships can be readily developed with suppliers in order to leverage skills and resources that are unobtainable by competitors. However, rather than using collaboration to achieve competitive advantage, the organisation that participated in this research used collaboration to build flexibility into the relationship and compensate for any gaps in the contract in order to react to changing circumstances or performance problems. It was often necessary to reconfigure and change the relationship between outsourced processes and internal processes. As evidenced from the cheque clearing case, collaboration acted as an important mechanism for dealing with performance difficulties without having to renegotiate the contract. Collaboration was an important mechanism for dealing with difficulties in the early phases of an outsourcing arrangement.

A limitation of the research undertaken has been applying the outsourcing framework in a single organisational setting. Further research is required in order to test the validity of the framework in a number of settings in order to generate additional insights into performance management and the outsourcing process. Although the experiences of the focal organisation in this research provide valuable insights, further research is required in organisations that have more mature outsourcing strategies. There were latent political influences on some of the outsourcing processes studied. Organisational politics involves the strategies that individuals employ in order to obtain and use power to influence organisational goals in order to further their own interests and ambitions (McIvor, 2005). This is an area of outsourcing research, which requires further examination. In particular, it would be valuable to carry out in-depth case study analysis to understand more fully the relationship between the political behaviour and outsourcing performance.

The research focused primarily on the area of performance management in an outsourcing context, primarily through using the resource-based view as a theoretical lens. However, there is potential to integrate Transaction Cost Economics with the resource-based view to understand more fully the link between risk and performance in outsourcing. Performance and risk are closely linked in the outsourcing process. Difficulties with specifying and assessing performance levels associated with processes increase the risks associated with outsourcing. Performance measurement difficulties can create the potential for each party to the relationship to renege on their requirements. Of course, one means of reducing the risks of performance measurement difficulties is to include more safeguards in the contract. For example, the contract can include clauses to allow third-party performance monitoring, the disclosure of documentation to verify that work has been completed and benchmarks to assess performance. However, business improvement techniques such as workflow mapping can be used to improve process performance and risks in outsourcing relationships. Workflow mapping can be employed to remove inefficiencies and idiosyncratic requirements from processes both prior to transferring them to service providers and during the outsourcing relationship. Further research is required in this area in order to explore more fully how business improvement techniques can be integrated into the outsourcing process both to enhance performance and reduce risks. In addition, employing the resource-based view and TCE as theoretical frameworks would further assist with this analysis.

Chapter 7

Conclusion and Management Implications

Outsourcing remains a live issue for strategic decision makers. This book has examined the issue of performance measurement in the outsourcing process. The research was undertaken with a UK FSO. The research focused on a number of processes that this organisation had outsourced and examined how performance measurement considerations could be better integrated with the outsourcing process. Furthermore, the research examined a number of processes that the organisation had identified as potential outsourcing candidates in order to better understand the range of potential sourcing options involved, which ranged from invest to improve internally to total outsourcing. The findings from the research have a number of important implications for practitioners.

■ The outsourcing decision-making process must be linked with the overall business strategy of the organisation. Understanding current performance and the degree to which sustainable superior performance in a process can be maintained enables the outsourcing process to be linked with the overall strategy of the organisation. Although this type of analysis is extremely challenging for organisations, it can be very valuable. The importance and depth of this analysis has been illustrated clearly in the case of organisational capability analysis. For example, crucial strategic information is obtained in the comparison of internal performance capabilities with the capabilities of service providers. In particular, the capability of an organisation in critical processes is the key to building and sustaining competitive advantage.

■ Assessing the relative importance of organisational processes via the CSF method is a valuable technique that can assist in outsourcing decision making. As well as linking outsourcing evaluation with the factors in the business environment that underpin organisational success, the CSF method provides a mechanism and language for prioritising which processes require attention either through internal improvement or outsourcing.

■ Organisations must have robust performance measurement systems in place in order to effectively evaluate and manage the outsourcing process. Effective performance measurement can assist in identifying causes of poor performance prior to outsourcing. Furthermore, outsourcing processes without developing effective performance measures means an organisation will not know whether service providers are executing processes better or worse than the internal departments.

■ Organisations must have a clear understanding of the relationship and inter-dependencies between business processes prior to outsourcing. Failure to understand the inter-dependencies between internal and outsourced processes can make supplier performance assessment an extremely difficult task.

■ Although internal process analysis can be time consuming, more effective outsourcing decisions can be made. Rather than outsourcing disparate and poorly performing processes, redesigning internal processes prior to outsourcing can enable an organisation to define clear boundaries between processes that should be internalised and those that should be outsourced.

■ Understanding clearly the nature of processes prior to outsourcing is an important pre-requisite for successful performance management with the supplier. Detailed requirements analysis will facilitate the development of an effective SLA, which can be used to measure supplier performance. Therefore, performance in an outsourcing relationship needs to be defined, measured and managed in order to achieve desired objectives.

■ Considerable investment of staff time is necessary in order to implement the outsourcing arrangement both during the evaluation phase and once the contract has been signed. Staff will be required for objective setting, supplier training, performance management and joint problem solving.

■ Care should be taken when developing the SLA so that it can be used as a practical day-to-day tool to measure performance. The emphasis should be on meeting strategic objectives rather than imposing penalties on the supplier. Adequate attention must also be paid to frequency of measurement in the SLA.

■ When designing an SLA, an organisation should consider the impact of allowing the service provider to focus its service delivery and performance management exclusively on the metrics within the agreement. It is likely that there may be gaps in the SLA, which need to be amended over time. Therefore, the SLA should be flexible enough to enable updating performance metrics on an agreed basis between client and service provider.

References

Abramovsky, L., Griffith, R. and Sako, M. (2004). Offshoring of Business Services and its Impact on the UK Economy, *AIM Research Working Paper Series*, 1–35.

Accounting Standards Board (ASB) (1994). *FRS 5: Reporting the Substance of Transactions*, London, UK, ASB.

Accounting Standards Committee (ASC) (1984). *SSAP 21: Accounting for Leases and Hire Purchase Contracts*, London, UK, ASC.

Anderson, S.W. and Dekker, H.C. (2005). Management control for market transactions: the relation between transaction characteristics, incomplete contract design, and subsequent performance, *Management Science*, 51, 12, 1734–1752.

Aron, R. and Singh, J.V. (2005). Getting offshoring right, *Harvard Business Review*, December, 135–143.

ASB (1998). *Amendment to FRS 5, Reporting the Substance of Transactions: The Private Finance Initiative and Similar Contracts*, London, UK, ASB.

Aubert, B., Rivard, S. and Patry, M. (1996). A transaction cost approach to outsourcing behaviour: some empirical evidence, *Information and Management*, 30, 51–64.

Barney, J.B. (1991). Firm resources and sustained competitive advantage, *Journal of Management*, 17, 1, 99–120.

Barney, J.B. (1999). How a firm's capabilities affect boundary decisions, *Sloan Management Review*, 40, 3, 137–145.

Barthelemy, J. (2001). The hidden costs of outsourcing, *Sloan Management Review*, Spring, 60–69.

Barthelemy, J. (2003). The seven deadly sins of outsourcing, *The Academy of Management Executive*, 17, 2, 87–98.

Barthelemy, J. and Geyer, D. (2000). IT outsourcing: findings from an empirical survey in France and Germany, *European Management Journal*, 19, 2, 195–202.

Bassett, R. (1991). Make-or-buy decisions, *Management Accounting*, November, 58–59.

Bettis, R.A., Bradley, S.P. and Hamel, G. (1992). Outsourcing and Industrial Decline, *Academy of Management Executive*, 6, 1, 7–22.

Blinder, A. (2006). Offshoring, *Foreign Affairs*, 85, 2, 113.

Blumberg, D.F. (1998). Strategic assessment of outsourcing and downsizing in the service market, *Managing Service Quality*, 8, 1, 5–18.

Boddy, D., Cahill, C., Charles, M., Fraser-Jraus, H. and MacBeth, D. (1998). Success and Failure in Implementing Supply Chain Partnering: An Empirical Study, *European Journal of Purchasing and Supply Chain Management*, 2, 2/3, 143–151.

Bryce, D.J. and Usseem, M. (1998). The impact of corporate outsourcing on company value, *The European Management Journal*, 16, 6, 635–643.

Burdon, S. and Bhalla, A. (2005). Lessons from the untold success story: outsourcing engineering and facilities management, *European Management Journal*, 13, 5, 576–582.

Caldwell, B. (2002). Outsourcing cost reduction creates paradox: how to still make a profit. *Gartner Dataquest Report*, CT, April 12.

Carpinetti, L.C.R. and de Melo, A.M. (2002). What to Benchmark? A Systematic Approach and Cases, *Benchmarking: An International Journal*, 9, 3, 244–255.

Casani, F., Luque, M.A., Luque, J. and Soria, P. (1996). La problematica del outsourcing, *Economistas*, 72, 86–98.

Croxton, K.L., Garcia-Dastugue, S.J., Lambert, D.M. and Rogers, D.L. (2001). The supply chain management process, *The International Journal of Logistics Management*, 12, 2, 13–36.

Culliton, J.W. (1956). Make or buy: a consideration of the problems fundamental to a decision whether to manufacture or buy materials, accessory equipment, fabricating parts and suppliers.

Das, T. and Teng, B. (2000). A resource-based theory of strategic alliances, *Journal of Management*, 26, 31–61.

Davenport, T. (2005). The Coming Commoditization of Processes, *Harvard Business Review*, June, 100–108.

Davison, D. (2004). Top ten risks of offshore outsourcing, *Meta Group Report*.

De Kok, A.G. and Graves, S.C. (2006). *Handbooks in Operations Research and Management Science Volume 12, Supply Chain Management, Design, Coordination and Operation*, Amsterdam, North Holland Publishing Company.

De Toni, A. and Tonchia, S. (2001). Performance measurement systems: models, characteristics and measures, *International Journal of Operations and Production Management*, 21, 46–70.

Deloitte Consulting. (2005) Calling a change in the outsourcing market: the realities for the world's largest organisations, April 2005, www.deloitte.com.

DiRomualdo, A. and Gurbaxani, V. (1998). Strategic intent for outsourcing, *Sloan Management Review*, 39, 4, 67–80.

Dyer, J.H. (1996). Specialised supplier networks as a source of competitive advantage: evidence from the auto industry, *Strategic Management Journal*, 17, 271–292.

Dyer, J.H. and Singh, H. (1998). The relational view: co-operative strategy and sources of interorganizational competitive advantage, *Academy of Management Review*, 23, 4, 660–679.

Earl, M.J. (1996). The risks of outsourcing IT, *Sloan Management Review*, 37, 3, 26–32.

Eisenhardt, K. (1989). Building theories from case study research, *Academy of Management Review*, 14, 4, 532–550.

Ellis, G. (1992). Make-or-buy decisions: a simpler approach, *Management Accounting*, June, 22–23.

Espino-Rodriguez, T. and Padron-Robaina, V. (2006). A review of outsourcing from the resource-based view, *International Journal of Management Reviews*, 8, 1, 49.

European Commission (1999). Implementing the framework for financial markets: action plan, FSAP [COM(1999) 232], Brussels.

Evans, P. and Wurster, T.S. (1999). *Blown to Bits: How the New Economics of Information Transforms Strategy*, Harvard Business School Press.

Foot, J. (1998). *How to Do Benchmarking: A Practitioner's Guide*, Inter Authorities Group, London.

Francheschini, F., Galetto, M., Pignatelli, A. and Varetto, M. (2003). Outsourcing: Guidelines for a Structured Approach, *Benchmarking: An International Journal*, 10, 3, 246–260.

Frei, F. and Harker, P.T. (1999). Measuring the efficiency of service delivery processes: an application to retail banking, *Journal of Service Research*, 1, 300–312.

Gainey, T.W. and Klaas, B.S. (2003). The outsourcing of training and development: factors impacting client satisfaction, *Journal of Management*, 29, 2, 207–229.

Gambino, A.J. (1980). The Make-or-buy Decision, *National Association of Accountants and the Society of Management Accountants*, Canada.

Gilley, K.M. and Rasheed, A. (2000). Making more by doing less: an analysis of outsourcing and its effects on firm performance, *Journal of Management*, 26, 4, 763–790.

Gottfredson, M., Puryear, R. and Phillips, S. (2005). Strategic sourcing: from periphery to the core, *Harvard Business Review*, February, 132–139.

Hagel, J. and Singer, M. (1999). Unbundling the corporation, *Harvard Business Review*, 77, 2, 133–142.

Hamel, G. and Prahalad, C.K. (1994). *Competing for the Future*, Boston, MA, Harvard Business Press.

Hammer, M. (2002). Process management and the future of six sigma, *Sloan Management Review*, Winter, 26–32.

Hardaker, M. and Ward, B.K. (1987). Getting things done, *Harvard Business Review*, 65, 6, 112–120.

Harland, C., Knight, L., Lamming, R. and Walker, H. (2005). Outsourcing: assessing the risks and benefits for organisations, sectors and nations, *International Journal of Operations and Production Management*, 25, 9, 831–850.

Helper, S., MacDuffie, J.P. and Sabel, C. (2000). Pragmatic collaborations: advancing knowledge while controlling opportunism, *Industrial and Corporate Change*, 9, 3, 443–488.

Higgins, C. (1955). Make-or-buy re-examined, *Harvard Business Review*, 33, 3, 109–119.

Ho, V.T., Ang, S. and Straub, D. (2003). When subordinates become IT contractors: persistent managerial expectations in IT outsourcing, *Information Systems Research*, 14, 1, 66–87.

Holcomb, T.R. and Hitt, M.A. (2007). Toward a model of strategic outsourcing, *Journal of Operations Management*, 25, 2, 464–481.

Insinga, R.C. and Werle, M.J. (2000). Linking outsourcing to business strategy, *Academy of Management Executive*, 14, 4, 58–70.

International Accounting Standards Board (IASB) (2004). *Press Release – 2 December 2004*, London, UK, IASB.

Kannan, V.R. and Tan, K.C. (2002). Supplier selection and assessment: their impact upon business performance, *The Journal of Supply Chain Management*, 38, 3, 11–21.

Kern, T., Willcocks, L. and Lacity, M. (2002). Application service provision: risk assessment and motivation, *MIS Quarterly Executive*, 1, 2, 113–126.

Kessler, I., Coyle-Shapiro, J. and Purcell, J. (1999). Outsourcing and the Employee Perspective, *Human Resource Management Journal*, 9, 2, 5–19.

Klaas, B.S., McClendon, J.A. and Gainey, T.W. (2001). Outsourcing HR: the impact of organisational characteristics, *Human Resource Management*, 40, 2, 125–138.

Krause, D.R., Pagell, M. and Curkovic, S. (2001). Toward a measure of competitive priorities for purchasing, *Journal of Operations Management*, 19, 4, 497–512.

Kripalani, M. and Engardio, P. (2003). The rise of India, *Business Week*, December, 38–46.

Lacity, M., Willcocks, L. and Feeny, D. (2004). Commercialising the back office at Lloyds of London: outsourcing and strategic partnerships revisited, *European Management Journal*, 22, 2, 127–140.

Lancellotti, R., Schein, O., Spang, S. and Stadler, V. (2003). ICT and operations outsourcing in banking insights from an interview-based pan-European survey *Wirtschafts Informatik*, http://www.wirtschaftsinformatik.de.

Langfield-Smith, K. and Smith, D. (2003). Management control systems and trust in outsourcing relationships, *Management Accounting Research*, 14, 3, 281–307.

Larson, K.D. (1998). The role of service level agreements in IT service delivery, *Information Management and Security*, 6, 3, 128–132.

Lei, D. and Hitt, M. (1995). Strategic restructuring and outsourcing, *Journal of Management*, 21, 835–859.

Linder, J. (2004). *Outsourcing for Radical Change: A Bold Approach to Enterprise Transformation*, Amacom, New York.

Lorenzoni, G. and Lipparini, A. (1999). The leveraging of inter-firm relationships as a distinctive organisational capability: a longitudinal study, *Strategic Management Journal*, 20, 4, 317–338.

Loveday, G. (1991). A PE 2 guide to creative accounting and SSAP 21, *Accountancy*, September, 71–72.

Mani, D., Barua, A. and Whinston, A.B. (2005). Of process analysis and alignment: a model of governance in BPO relationships, *University of Texas at Austin working paper*.

Mani, D., Barua, A. and Whinston, A. (2006). Successfully governing business process outsourcing relationships, *MIS Quarterly Executive*, 5, 1, 15–29.

Marshall, D., McIvor, R. and Lamming, R. (2007). Influences on outsourcing and outcomes: insights from the telecommunications industry, *Journal of Purchasing and Supply Management*, 13, 4, 245–260.

Matthews, J. (2003). Strategizing by firms in the presence of markets for resources, *Industrial and Corporate Change*, 12, 1157–1193.

McCarthy, I. and Anagnostou, A. (2004). The impact of outsourcing on the transaction costs and boundaries of manufacturing, *International Journal of Production Economics*, 1, 8, 61–71.

McFarlan, F.W. and Nolan, R.L. (1995). How to manage an IT outsourcing alliance, *Sloan Management Review*, 36, 2, 9–24.

McIvor, R. (2000). A practical framework for understanding the outsourcing process, *Supply Chain Management: An International Journal*, 5, 1, 22–36.

McIvor, R. (2005). *The Outsourcing Process: Strategies for Evaluation and Management*, Cambridge, MA, Cambridge University Press.

McIvor, R. (2007). Outsourcing and the spin-off arrangement: lessons from a utility company, *Journal of General Management*, 33, 1, 51–70.

McIvor, R. (2008). What is the right outsourcing strategy for your process?, *European Management Journal*, 26, 25–35.

McIvor, R. and McHugh, M. (2002). The organisational change implications of outsourcing, *The Journal of General Management*, 27, 4, Summer, 27–48.

Metters, R. and Verma, R. (2007). History of offshoring knowledge services, *Journal of Operations Management*, 26, 2, 141–147.

Mills, J., Platts, K. and Bourne, M. (2003). Applying resource-based theory: methods, outcomes and utility for managers, *International Journal of Operations and Production Management*, 23, 2, 148–166.

Mol, M.J., Van Tulder, R.J.M. and Beije, P.R. (2005). Antecedents and performance consequences of international outsourcing, *International Business Review*, 14, 599–617.

Nairn, G. (2003). A New Chapter for Outsourcing, *FT Understanding Business Agility Part 2*, London, Financial Times, 4–5.

Narayanan, V.G. and Raman, A. (2004). Aligning incentives in supply chains, *Harvard Business Review*, 82, 11, 94–102.

Nelson Hall (2006). Available from: http://www.nelson-hall.com/ [Accessed 15th December 2006].

Nelson Hall Report (2005). BPO Opportunities in the Banking Sector Marketing Assessment, August, UK.

Nelson Hall Report (2007). BPO Opportunities in the Banking Sector Marketing Assessment, August, UK.

Ngwenyama, O. and Bryson, N. (1999). Making the information systems outsourcing decision: a transaction cost approach to analysing outsourcing decision problems, *European Journal of Operational Research*, 115, 351–367.

Olsen, R.F. and Ellram, L.M. (1997). A portfolio approach to supplier relationships, *Industrial Marketing Management*, 26, 101–113.

Parkinson, J. (2004). Economic value added: does it add value? *International Accountant*, May, 36–38.

Peteraf, M.A. (1993). The cornerstones of competitive advantage: a resource-based view, *Strategic Management Journal*, 14, 179–191.

Poppo, L. and Zenger, T. (2002). Do formal contracts and relational governance function as substitutes or compliments? *Strategic Management Journal*, 23, 8, 707–725.

Porter, M.E. (2001). Strategy and the Internet, *Harvard Business Review*, 79, 2, 63–78.

Prahalad, C.K. and Hamel, G. (1990). The Core Competence of the Corporation, *Harvard Business Review*, July–August, 79–91.

Quelin, B. and Duhamel, F. (2003). Bringing together strategic outsourcing and corporate strategy: outsourcing motives and risks, *European Management Journal*, 21, 5, 647–661.

Quinn, J.B. (1999). Strategic outsourcing: leveraging knowledge capabilities, *Sloan Management Review*, 40, 4, 9–21.

Quinn, J.B. and Hilmer, F.G. (1994). Strategic outsourcing, *Sloan Management Review*, 35, 4, 43–55.

Robinson, M. and Kalakota, R. (2004). *Offshore Outsourcing: Business Models, ROI and Best Practices*, Mivar Press.

Rockart, J.F. (1979). Chief Executives define their own data needs, *Harvard Business Review*, 57, 2, 81–92.

Rottman, J. and Lacity, M. (2004). Proven practices for IT offshore outsourcing, *Cutters Consortium Report*, 5, 12, 1–27.

Sako, M. (2006). Outsourcing and offshoring: implications for productivity of business services, *Oxford Review of Economic Policy*, 22, 4, 499–512.

Shi, Y. (2007). Today's solution and tomorrow's problem: the business process outsourcing risk and management puzzle, *California Management Review*, 49, 3, 27–44.

Shin, H., Collier, D.A. and Wilson, D.D. (2000). Supply management orientation and supplier/buyer performance, *Journal of Operations Management*, 18, 3, 317–333.

Silver, E.A. (2004). Process management instead of operations management, *Manufacturing and Service Operations Management*, 6, 4, 273–279.

Skinner, W. (1969). Manufacturing – missing link in corporate strategy, *Harvard Business Review*, May–June, 136–144.

Skogstad, E. (2004). Using Benchmark Metrics to Uncover Best Practice, *Business Credit*, 106, 1, 54–55.

Slack, N. and Lewis, M. (2002). *Operations Strategy*, London, UK, Prentice Hall.

Spekman, R.E. and Davis, E.W. (2004). Risky business: expanding the discussion on risk and the extended enterprise, *International Journal of Physical Distribution and Logistics Management*, 34, 5, 414–433.

Stern, S. (2000). Stern Stewart roundtable on EVA and corporate outsourcing, *Journal of Applied Corporate Finance*, 13, 1, 88–107.

Stewart, G.B. (1991). *Quest for Value*, New York, HarperCollins.

Stringer, E. (1996). *Action Research: A Handbook for Practitioners*, Thousand Oaks, CA, Sage.

Teng, J.T.C., Cheon, M.J. and Grover, V. (1995). Decisions to outsource information systems functions: testing a strategy-theoretic-discrepancy model, *Decision Sciences*, 26, 1, 75–103.

TPI (2007). HRO transformation: myth or reality, *TPI Report*, 1–23.

Van Veen-Dirks, P. and Wijn, M. (2002). Strategic control: meshing critical success factors with the balanced scorecard, *Long Range Planning*, 35, 407–427.

Venkatesan, R. (1992). Strategic sourcing: to make or not to make, *Harvard Business Review*, 70, 6, 98–107.

Vining, A. and Globerman, S. (1999). A conceptual framework for understanding the outsourcing decision, *European Management Journal*, 17, 6, 645–654.

Ward, B. (1990). Planning for profit, in Lincoln, T. (Ed) *Managing Information Systems for Profit*, Chichester, UK, Wiley.

Webb, L. and Laborde, J. (2005). Crafting a successful outsourcing vendor/client relationship, *Business Process Management Journal*, 11, 5, 437–443.

Welch, J.A. and Nayak, P.R. (1992). Strategic sourcing: a progressive approach to the make-or-buy decision, *Academy of Management Executive*, 6, 1, 23–31.

Williamson, O.E. (1975). *Markets and Hierarchies*, New York, Free Press.

Williamson, O.E. (1985). *The Economic Institutions of Capitalism: Firms, Markets and Relational Contracting*, New York, Free Press.

Wisniewski, M. (2001). Measuring up to the best: a manager's guide to benchmarking, *Exploring Public Sector Strategy*, London, UK, Prentice Hall, pp. 84–110.

Womack, J., Jones, D.T. and Roos, D. (1990). *The Machine that Changed the World*, New York, Rawson Associates.

Youngdahl, W. et al (2007). Exploring new frontiers in offshoring knowledge and service process, *Journal of Operation Management*, 26, 2, 135–140.

Youngdahl, W. and Ramaswamy, K. (2008). Offshoring Knowledge and Service Work: A Conceptual Model and Research Agenda, *Journal of Operations Management*, 26, 2, 212–221.

Appendices

Appendix 1

Sample Workflow Chart for the Mortgages Process

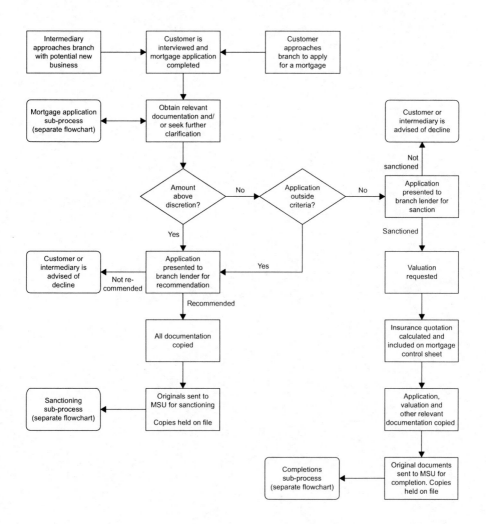

Appendix 2

Workflow Chart for the Encoding Sub-Process

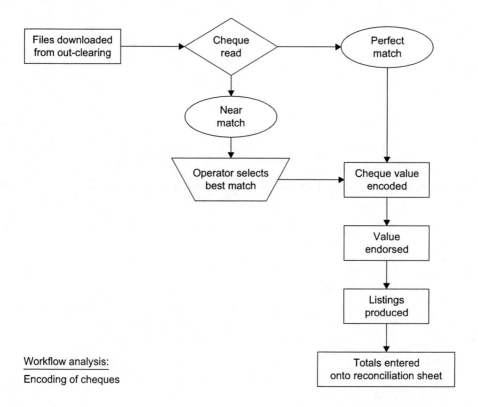

Files downloaded from out-clearing → Cheque read → Perfect match

Cheque read → Near match → Operator selects best match → Cheque value encoded

Perfect match → Cheque value encoded → Value endorsed → Listings produced → Totals entered onto reconciliation sheet

Workflow analysis:

Encoding of cheques

Appendix 3

Category	Criteria	KPI	Required activity level
Outclearing	Quality	Items to be sorted into required categories	99%
	Quality	Number of unmatched items against the number that should have been matched	
	Timeliness	Collection of orange bags – following delivery of work, each of the branch bags will be checked to ensure that they are empty and ready for collection by 21:00 hours	
	Timeliness	Outclearing will be ready for collection by courier at 23:30 hours	
Debit in-clearing	Quality	Receipt of all exchange items and high-level balancing	99%

(Continued)

Category	Criteria	KPI	Required activity level
	Quality	All code lines for each item to be captured on day of receipt	95%
	Quality	All capture files transmitted correctly to mainframe to enable updating with exception code	99%
	Timeliness	Capture files to be transmitted regularly during the day up to an agreed cut-off time of 16:00 hours	
	Timeliness	Presentation of work – all items boxed and labelled for collection at 15:30 hours	
Credit referencing	Quality	All visa envelopes opened and prepared for processing	95%
	Quality	All cheques to have customer reference number noted on the back of the cheque	95%
	Timeliness	All postal cheques for processing to be ready for pick-up at 10:00, 11:00, 14:00 and 15:00 hours	
	Timeliness	Data file transmitted to the mainframe to agreed timescale. Transmission completed by 17:00 hours on a daily basis	

(*Continued*)

Category	Criteria	KPI	Required activity level
Settlement	Quality	Completion of the settlement process and feedback	97%
	Timeliness	Queries relating to the days exchange figures resolved within 1 hour	
	Quality	All applications must be balanced to show zero total = completion of control reports	
	Timeliness	Reports to be received within agreed time frame. Final exchange summary ready for collection at 14:00 hours	
	Timeliness	Instructions to be actioned relative to the provider account on the next working day	
	Timeliness	Transfers to be completed by 13:00 hours on the next working day	

Appendix 4

Performance of the Debit In-Clearing Sub-Process

	Quality					Timeliness			Cost
	Receipt of all exchange items and high-level balancing	All code lines for each item to be captured on day of receipt – FSO 1	All code lines for each item to be captured on day of receipt – FSO 2	All capture files transmitted correctly to mainframe to enable updating with exception code – FSO 1	All capture files transmitted correctly to mainframe to enable updating with exception code – FSO 2	Capture files to be transmitted by customary cut-off time – FSO 1	Capture files to be transmitted by customary cut-off time – FSO 2	Capture files to be transmitted by new target cut-off time – FSO 2	Overtime used (Target = 0%)
0–6 months	95%	97%	86%	97%	81%	95%	99%	–	15%
	95%	97%	86%	97%	81%	95%	99%	–	15%
	95%	97%	86%	97%	81%	95%	99%	–	15%
	95%	97%	86%	97%	81%	95%	99%	–	15%
	95%	97%	86%	97%	81%	95%	99%	–	15%
	95%	97%	86%	97%	81%	95%	99%	–	15%
	97%	97%	93%	97%	81%	97%	99%	–	15%
	97%	99%	93%	97%	81%	97%	99%	–	15%
7–9 months	97%	99%	93%	97%	81%	97%	99%	–	15%
	99%	99%	93%	97%	81%	90%	97%	–	15%

9–15 months	99%	99%	93%	97%	81%	90%	97%	—	15%
	99%	99%	93%	97%	81%	90%	97%	—	15%
	99%	99%	96%	97%	81%	90%	99%	—	10%
	99%	99%	96%	97%	81%	90%	99%	—	10%
	99%	99%	96%	97%	81%	90%	99%	—	10%
15–24 months	99%	99%	96%	97%	88%	92%	—	70%	15%
	99%	99%	96%	97%	88%	92%	—	70%	15%
	99%	99%	96%	97%	88%	95%	—	75%	20%
	99%	99%	96%	97%	88%	95%	—	75%	20%
	99%	99%	96%	97%	88%	95%	—	75%	20%
	99%	99%	96%	97%	88%	95%	—	75%	20%
	99%	99%	96%	97%	88%	95%	—	80%	20%
	99%	99%	96%	97%	88%	95%	—	80%	15%
	99%	99%	96%	97%	88%	97%	—	80%	15%
	99%	99%	96%	97%	88%	97%	—	90%	15%
	99%	99%	96%	97%	88%	97%	—	90%	10%
	99%	99%	96%	97%	88%	97%	—	90%	10%

(Continued)

	Quality					Timeliness			Cost
	Receipt of all exchange items and high-level balancing	All code lines for each item to be captured on day of receipt – FSO 1	All code lines for each item to be captured on day of receipt – FSO 2	All capture files transmitted correctly to mainframe to enable updating with exception code – FSO 1	All capture files transmitted correctly to mainframe to enable updating with exception code – FSO 2	Capture files to be transmitted by customary cut-off time – FSO 1	Capture files to be transmitted by customary cut-off time – FSO 2	Capture files to be transmitted by new target cut-off time – FSO 2	Overtime used (Target = 0%)
24–30 months	99%	99%	96%	97%	93%	97%	–	90%	10%
	99%	99%	96%	97%	93%	97%	–	90%	5%
	99%	99%	96%	97%	93%	97%	–	90%	5%
	99%	99%	96%	97%	93%	97%	–	92%	5%
	99%	99%	96%	97%	93%	97%	–	92%	5%
	99%	99%	96%	97%	93%	97%	–	92%	0%
30–36 months	99%	99%	96%	97%	96%	97%	–	92%	0%
	99%	99%	96%	97%	96%	97%	–	92%	0%
	99%	99%	96%	97%	96%	97%	–	92%	0%

Index

Lightning Source UK Ltd.
Milton Keynes UK
UKOW041136020812

196924UK00004B/31/P